# Tipbook
# Saxophone
*The Complete Guide*

Hugo Pinksterboer

# Tipbook
# Saxophone
*The Complete Guide*

THE **TIPBOOK**
**COMPANY**

## The Best Guide To Your Instrument!
www.tipbook.com

## Publishing details

This third edition published January 2007 by
The Tipbook Company bv, The Netherlands.
Distributed exclusively by the Hal Leonard Corporation,
7777 West Bluemound Road, P.O. Box 13819
Milwaukee, Wisconsin 53213.

The publisher and author have done their best to ensure the accuracy and timeliness of all the information in this Tipbook; however, they can accept no responsibility for any loss, injury, or inconvenience sustained as a result of information or advice contained in this book. Trademarks, user names, and certain illustrations have been used in this book solely to identify the products or instruments discussed. Such use does not imply endorsement by or affiliation with the trademark owner(s).

ISBN 10: 90-8767-101-6
ISBN 13: 978-90-8767-101-3
EAN: 9789087671013

# Thanks!

For their information, their expertise, their time, and their help, we'd like to thank the following musicians, teachers, technicians, and other saxophone experts:

Terry Landry (Rico International, CA), Tim Brennan, James Grondin (The Woodwind & Brasswind, IN), Ray Chambers (American Band Instrument Service, TX), Roberto Romeo (Roberto's Winds, NY), Thierry Lobel (Selmer, France), Candy Dulfer, Hans Dulfer, Leo van Oostrom, Davina Cowan, Fred Leeflang, Josephine van Rosmalen, Gerdie IJland, Hans Jan van der Deure and Paul Kortenhorst (Saxophone Shop), Louis Hummel (Hummel Saxophones), Wim Tober (LVSD/National Association of Saxophone Teachers), Gerard ten Hoedt (Müller Music), Hanneke van der Horst, Willem Pinksterboer, and the late Peter Barkema.

## The makers

Journalist and musician **Hugo Pinksterboer**, author and editor of *The Tipbook Series*, has published hundreds of interviews, articles, and instrument, video, CD, and book reviews for national and international music magazines.

Illustrator, designer, and musician **Gijs Bierenbroodspot** has worked as an art director for a wide variety of magazines and has developed numerous ad campaigns. While searching in vain for information about saxophone mouthpieces, he got the idea for this series of books on music and musical instruments. He is responsible for the layout and illustrations of all of the Tipbooks.

## Acknowledgements

Concept, design, and illustrations: Gijs Bierenbroodspot
Cover photo: René Vervloet
Editors: Robert L. Doerschuk and Michael J. Collins
Proofreaders: Nancy Bishop and René de Graaff

## Anything missing?

Any omissions? Any areas that could be improved? Please go to www.tipbook.com to contact us; thanks!

# Contents

# *In brief*

**Have you just started playing the saxophone? Are you thinking about buying a sax, or do you just want to learn more about the one you already have? If so, this book will tell you all you need to know. About buying or renting saxophones, lessons and practicing, play-testing and selecting an instrument, choosing mouthpieces, reeds, and ligatures, maintenance and tuning, about the history and the family of the saxophone, and much more.**

### *The best you can*
Having read this Tipbook, you'll be able to get the best out of your saxophone, to buy the best instrument you can, and to easily grasp any other literature on the subject, from books and magazines to catalogs and Internet publications.

### *Basics*
The first five chapters are meant for beginners only — or their parents. They explain the basics of the instrument and the different saxophone voices, and inform you on learning to play the saxophone, practicing, and buying or renting an instrument. This information also fully prepares you to read the rest of the book.

### *Advanced players*
Advanced players can skip ahead to Chapter 6, where you find everything you need to know to make an informed purchase

when you're going to buy a saxophone. Chapters 7 and 8 offer similar information on selecting mouthpieces, ligatures, and reeds. Chapter 8 also covers reed adjustment tips!

## Maintenance
Everything to get the best out of your instrument can be found in Chapters 9 and 10, covering tuning, assembly, accessories, cleaning, maintenance, and related subjects.

## Background information
The final chapters offer essential reading material on the history of the saxophone, the family of the instrument, its production, and the main brand names that you'll come across.

## US dollars
Please note that all price indications listed on the following pages are based on estimated street prices in American dollars.

## Glossary
The glossary at the end of the book briefly explains most of the terms you'll come across as a sax player. Also included are an index of terms, and a couple of pages for essential notes on your equipment.

## Tipbook fingering charts
Many readers of earlier editions of Tipbook Saxophone asked us to include fingering charts — and so we did. True: You can find fingering charts on the Internet also, but a book is easier to take along (and you don't have to turn it on either). Besides, the Tipbook Fingering Charts are presented in a very clear way, showing all relevant fingerings for each note on a double page, so you don't have to go back and forth to compare various fingerings. False fingerings are included, of course. Enjoy!

## Hugo Pinksterboer

# See and hear what you read with Tipcode

*www.tipbook.com*

**In addition to the many illustrations on the following pages, Tipbooks offer you a new way to see — and hear! — what you are reading about. The Tipcodes that you will come across throughout this book give you access to short videos, sound files, and other additional information at www.tipbook.com.**

Here is how it works: On page 19 of this book there's a paragraph on the different registers of a saxophone. Below that paragraph is a short section on **Tipcode SAX-003**. Type in this code on the Tipcode page at www.tipbook.com and the saxophone's registers will be demonstrated for you.

TIPCODE

**Tipcode SAX-003**
Play this Tipcode to listen to the low, middle and upper registers of an alto saxophone.

## Enter code, watch video

You enter the Tipcode below the movie window on the Tipcode

page. In most cases, you'll see the relevant video and/or hear audio within five to ten seconds.

### Tipcodes listed

For your convenience, the Tipcodes presented in this book are also listed on page 176.

### Quick start

The videos and sound files are designed so that they start quickly. If you miss something the first time, you can of course repeat them. And if it all happens too fast, use the pause button below the movie window.

First, make your selection: Tipcode, chords and fingering charts, or the glossary.

The Tipcode window displays videos, fingering charts, chords, and explanations of the words used in this book.

Enter a Tipcode here and click on the button. Want to see it again? Click again.

These links take you directly to other interesting sites.

### Software

If the software you need to view the videos is not yet installed on your computer, you'll automatically be told which software you need, and where you can download it. This software is free. Questions? Check out 'About this site' at www.tipbook.com.

### Still more at www.tipbook.com

You can find even more information at www.tipbook.com. For instance, you can look up words in the glossaries of *all* the Tipbooks published to date. There are chord diagrams for guitarists and pianists; fingering charts for saxophonists, clarinetists, and flutists; and rudiments for drummers. Also included are links to most of the websites mentioned in the *Want to Know More?* section of each Tipbook.

# 1

# A Saxophonist?

*As a saxophonist you can play perfect, straight notes, and you can make your instrument whisper, scream, or hiss just as easily. That's one of the main reasons why you hear saxophonists play in a wide variety of musical styles, and in many different types of bands and orchestras.*

With a saxophone you can go from jazz to classical music, from Latin to rock and soul. As you can influence the sound of the instrument to a large extent, saxophonists can be equally at home in all those styles.

### High school and college bands
Of course, saxophonists are essential in all the various types of high school and college bands: marching bands that perform either onstage, in parades, or during football games; jazz bands; wind bands; or concert bands, which may have some sixty to more than a hundred band members.

### Rock, funk, jazz
You can also join the horn section of a rock or funk band, adding spicy riffs or tender harmonies to the music. Saxophone solos are rare in such bands, but they're one of the main features in jazz ensembles. Popular formats are the jazz quartet (saxophone, drums, piano, double bass) or quintet, which usually includes a second saxophonist or a trumpet player.

### Very young
You won't find the saxophone in the standard lineup of the symphony orchestra. Why not? Because Beethoven, Mozart, and numerous other great classical composers were long dead when Adolphe Sax invented the saxophone, around 1840. The other instruments in the symphony orchestra are a lot older.

### But you can play it
That's not to say that you can't play music from that era: Lots of compositions have been adapted for sax players. Composers of later date have also written classical music for saxophonists. Some well-known names are Béla Bartók, Hector Berlioz, Maurice Ravel, and Richard Strauss.

### Much more
Apart from a wide range of bands and orchestras, there are many other formats for sax players. For example, there are compositions for saxophone solo (just a sax, nothing else); there are duets for sax and piano, or for two saxophones (you can

2

use duets written for oboe or flute too, if you want to play older music!). Also, there is music for saxophone quartets, ranging from jazz and improvised music to hymns, children's songs, and string quartets that have been adapted for saxes. A similar range of works is available for saxophone choirs, a larger type of ensemble.

**TIP**

### Alto and tenor

Saxophones come in various sizes or *voices*. The *alto saxophone* and the larger, lower-sounding *tenor saxophone* are the most widely used. Their sounds suit all kinds of music, and they're easier to master than the other voices. Most players start on one of these horns.

**TIPCODE**

**Tipcode SAX-001**
In this Tipcode you'll hear the different timbres of alto and tenor saxophones.

### Soprano and baritone

The next two popular saxes are the small, high-pitched *soprano*,

3

and the big, low-pitched *baritone saxophone*. Saxophone players often specialize in one of the four voices — but they usually play two or more of them.

*A tenor (left) and an alto saxophone.*

### And more

There are even more saxophones; you'll find the others in Chapter 12, *The Family*. As different as they may appear, all saxophones are basically the exact same instrument, with the exact same arrangement of keys. It's only the sizes that differ.

### Saxes and horns

As 'saxophone' is quite a long word, most saxophonists talk about their 'sax' instead. Likewise, some musicians say 'saxist' rather than saxophonist. Many sax players call their instrument a 'horn' — just like trumpeters and other brass players often do.

# A quick tour

With all of those keys and rods, a saxophone looks more complicated than it really is. In this chapter you will see which parts make up a saxophone, what they're called and what they're for.

Each saxophone has basically the same set of parts, whether it's a soprano, an alto, a tenor, or a baritone. In this chapter, the alto saxophone is pictured. You'll find the others in the next chapter, *Four Saxes*.

### Tube with holes
Essentially, a saxophone is a long tube with holes in it. Just as on a recorder, you play the lowest note by closing off all of those *toneholes*. If you open the last hole, the tone goes up: You'll play a higher pitch. If you then open the next tonehole, the pitch is raised again — and so on.

### The keys
The toneholes of a saxophone are too far apart, and most of them are far too big, to cover them with your fingertips. Besides, there are more toneholes than you have fingers. That's why the instrument has *keys* to open and close them.

*A saxophone body and bell without its keys: a long tube full of holes.*

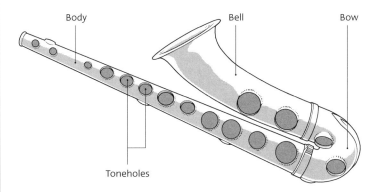

Body

Bell

Bow

Toneholes

### Body, neck, and bell
The largest part of a saxophone, covered with keys and rods, is the *body*. At the top end you'll find the *neck*. The wide flaring part at the other end is the *bell*.

### Mouthpiece and reed
Attached to the neck is the *mouthpiece* with the *reed*. This reed, a thin piece of cane, is what generates the saxophone sound. A *ligature* holds the reed in place.

6

Mouthpiece

Ligature

Neck

Body

Palm keys

Left-hand
little finger
keys

Rods

Side keys

Pearl keys

Right-hand
little finger
keys

Key guard

Bell

Key guard

Key cup

Bow

*The main parts
of a saxophone
(front).*

*The main parts of a saxophone (back).*

Reed

Octave key

Thumb rest

Left-hand little finger keys

Body

Hanger loop

Thumb hook (right thumb)

Key guard

Bow

## Sound

When you talk or sing, your vocal chords vibrate. This makes the air around them vibrate, and that's what sound is: vibrating air. When you are playing the sax, you make the reed vibrate, and with it the air column in the saxophone.

## Long tube, low notes

If you close all the toneholes, the saxophone will sound its lowest note: The sax 'tube' is at its longest. To play higher notes, you open one or more toneholes. The more toneholes you open, the higher notes will sound.

## Pads

In order for a sax to play well, its keys should properly close the toneholes, without any air leaking. Therefore, the *key cups* that stop the toneholes are fitted with *pads*. These felt discs, covered with thin, soft leather, seal the toneholes.

## Resonators

In the middle of each pad is a small metal or plastic disc. These *resonators* make the instrument sound a little brighter.

Key cup

Pad

Resonator

Key arm

Rod

## Wider and wider

The body of the sax becomes wider as it progresses from the neck to the bell. In technical terms, saxophones have a *conical shape* — like an ice-cream cone.

## Bigger and bigger
As the saxophone gets wider, the toneholes get bigger.

- The **smallest tonehole** is on the neck: It's the neck octave vent.
- The **largest tonehole** is located at the opposite end of the horn, in the bell.
- Some consider **the bell** itself to be the largest tonehole: That's where the lowest note comes from.

## Nine digits, twenty-five keys
The key system allows you to open and close all of the sax's twenty-four or twenty-five toneholes with just eight fingers and a thumb.

## Springs
When you're not playing, about half of the keys are open; the others are closed. Each key has a *needle spring*, which makes sure the key closes again after you've opened it, or the other way around.

## Felts and corks
Small felt and cork *bumpers* prevent the moving metal parts from producing too much noise. They also help some keys open and close simultaneously, and determine how far some of the keys open.

## Key guards
*Key guards* protect some of the most vulnerable key cups from getting damaged.

## Thumb hook, thumb rest
Your right thumb, placed under the *thumb hook*, helps support the instrument. Your left thumb, placed on the *thumb rest*, operates the *octave key*.

## Hanger loop
Saxophones are supported by a neckstrap or *sling*. The *hanger loop* for the strap hook is about halfway up the back of the body.

Upper
octave vent
(smallest
tonehole)

*The toneholes
are closed by key
cups. To play
the lowest tone
(low B♭), all
toneholes need
to be closed.*

Lower
octave
vent

High F♯

High F

High E

B

B♭

A

G

G♯

F

E

low B♭
(largest
tonehole)

D

Low B

Low C

Low C♯

11

*The toneholes are closed by key cups.*

Upper octave vent (smallest tonehole)

High F

High E♭

High D

C

B♭

F♯

Low E♭

# THE KEYS

Sax players use many different names for the keys of their instrument. What one calls a pearl key is a finger pad to the next, for example. Following are some of the main names.

### The system
The entire system of keys, springs, rods, and other moving parts, is referred to as the *keywork*, *key system*, *mechanism*, or *action*.

### Keys and key cups
Technically speaking, keys are the things you press to open or close a tonehole, while the key cups or *pad cups* actually stop the toneholes. Most saxophonists, however, use the word key for the entire system, from *key* to key cup.

---

**TIP**

> #### Easy
> The complex-looking mechanism of a saxophone becomes a lot easier to understand if you just look at the keys your fingers rest on, as shown on pages 16–17. To complete the picture, you'll find all the key cups and the corresponding notes on page 11.

---

### Pearl keys
The front side of the sax has eight round keys with a mother-of-pearl or (imitation) shell inlay. They're usually referred to as *pearl keys*, *key pearls*, or *pearls*. Some horns have such inlays on other keys as well.

### Little finger keys
Your left little finger operates no less than four keys. This takes a bit of practice, in the beginning. Your right little finger controls two similar keys. The rollers between the keys make it easier to slide your pinkie from one key to the other.

13

Rollers

### Alternative names
The little finger keys are also known as *table keys* or *touch plates*. The groups of two (right hand) and four (left hand) pinkie keys are also known as the *lower* and *upper stack*, respectively, and as (*floating rocker*) *tables*, *plateaus*, or *clusters*

### Side and palm keys
On the right-hand side you'll find four or five rectangular keys, the *side keys*. On the top left-hand side, there are three *palm keys*, so called because you can play them with the palm of your hand. These two sets of keys are mostly used for playing high notes and trills.

### Spatulas
Due to their shape, the front F key, and the side and palm keys are also known as *spatula keys* or *spatulas*. The little finger keys are sometimes referred to as spatulas too. Keys with a lever-type action are known as *levers*.

# KEYS AND NOTES

On a piano, there's a key for every note. On a saxophone, it's very different: For most notes, you need a combination of keys. That makes it hard to add note names to the keys.

14

### Londeix

Still, it's useful to be able to identify them. Over the years, a number of systems have been developed for this purpose. One of the most common, conceived by the French saxophonist Jean Marie Londeix, is pictured on the next two pages.

### Keys 1 to 8

The keys 1 to 6 are played with your right and left index, middle, and ring fingers. Your right little finger operates key 7 (for the low C) and the key for the low E-flat (E♭). Your left little finger operates key 8, on the upper stack.

### Octave key

Key O, on the back, is the octave key. If you play, say, a low G, and then press the octave key, you will hear a G that sounds an *octave* higher (eight white notes on a piano keyboard).

TIPCODE

**Tipcode SAX-002**
This Tipcode demonstrates the use of the octave key.

### Two vents

The octave key opens and closes two vents. The upper one is on the neck, clearly visible. The lower octave vent is on the body, between the high E and F♯ key cups (see page 11). You don't need to worry about which one to open for the note you're playing: You just operate the octave key, and the system automatically opens the right vent.

### The very highest

Keys C1 through C5 are for the highest notes. The higher the number, the higher the pitch of the note. C5 is for high F-sharp (F♯). Not all saxophones have this key (see pages 59–60).

15

Key names
according to Jean
Marie Londeix.

X — — C2
1 — — C1
P — — C4
2 —
3 —

C3 —
Tc —
Ta — — 4
C5 —
Tf — — 5
D♯ — — 6
7 —

O

G#
C#
8
B♭

### Trills and more

The keys named with a T are used to play trills, but not only that. One example? With Tc you can, of course, also just play a C. As for the trills:

• With Tc you can trill between B and C.
• With Tf you can trill between F and F♯.
• With Ta you can trill between A and B♭.

### F = X

Key X, also known as *front F*, *quick F*, or *forked F*, can be used to reach not only high F, but also high E and F♯ in certain passages.

*Fingering chart. By pressing the two shaded keys, you'll finger an A.*

## Fingering charts

*On a saxophone, most notes can be played with various fingerings. Fingering charts for all saxophone voices can be found on pages 187-211 of this Tipbook, or at www.tipbook.com.*

# THE REGISTERS

The octave key is also known as the *register key*: You use it to go from the lowest series of notes you can play (the low register) to the next, higher-sounding series (the middle register).

### Four registers

The range of the saxophone is typically divided into four registers.

- The low register encompasses the notes you play without using the octace key: from low A or B♭ (A3/B♭3) up to the C♯ that you play with all keys open (C♯5).
- The middle register: D5 to C♯6.
- The high register (D6 to F♯6) is played using the keys that are labeled C1 to C5 (see pages 16 and 17)
- The fourth register, the altissimo register, is for advanced players only. The notes of this particular register (toptones) are played using harmonics, which require special fingerings and air stream adjustments.

**Tipcode SAX-003**
Play this Tipcode to listen to the low, middle and upper registers of an alto saxophone.

**TIPCODE**

### Five registers

Some players distinguish five registers, the bottom register encompassing the four very lowest notes of the instrument (low B♭, B, C, and C♯), or the five lowest notes on baritones with a low A.

**19**

# 3

# Four saxes

*If you go to a store and ask for a saxophone, you will be
asked which voice you want: an alto, or a tenor, or perhaps a
soprano or a baritone? This chapter introduces you to these
four voices, their sound, and their ranges — and it explains
why a C is not always a C.*

From a distance, you might say that a baritone sax looks nothing like a soprano sax. However, they are basically the same instruments. The baritone is just bigger, and thus lower in pitch.

### Soprano

Because of its size, the high-sounding soprano sax is easy to handle. Sopranos are usually not recommended for beginning players, however, as these smaller horns are harder to play in tune than altos or tenors. Traditionally, sopranos have a straight body, but curved sopranos are available too.

*The range of a soprano saxophone*

***Tipcode SAX-004***
*This Tipcode demonstrates the sound and timbre of a soprano saxophone.*

### Alto

The alto sax is a better choice for beginners. It's easier to play in tune than a soprano, and easier to handle than a tenor. The alto is at home in pretty much any style of music, and there's more

*The range of an alto saxophone*

**22**

classical music written for the alto than for any of the other saxophone voices.

**Tipcode SAX-005**

Here you'll hear what an alto is capable of.

*Left: A soprano saxophone.*

*Right: An alto saxophone.*

### Tenor

The tenor is the most widely used sax in jazz, but you'll find it in other styles as well. The sound could be described as warmer, fatter, juicier, or richer than that of an alto or a soprano. It's also more versatile: You can make a tenor sound anywhere from piercing and edgy to soft as a whisper. Together with the alto, the tenor is the best choice for beginning players.

*The range of a tenor saxophone*

**TIPCODE**

**Tipcode SAX-006**
Listen to this Tipcode and you'll know what a tenor saxophone sounds like.

### Baritone

The baritone sax or *bari* is the largest of the four. To make it manageable, it has its typical looped neck and a 'tall' bell. If not, it would be over seven feet long. The baritone, with its big, fat tone, sounds an octave lower than the alto. It's not a great horn for beginners, due to its size and price.

*The range of a baritone saxophone*

24

### Tipcode SAX-007
This Tipcode demonstrates the characteristics of a baritone sax.

Left: A tenor saxophone.

Right: A baritone saxophone.

# HOW HIGH, HOW LOW?

The normal range of a saxophone is about two and a half octaves. Good players can stretch it to three or four octaves, or even further.

TIPCODE

**Tipcode SAX-008**
With this Tipcode, you'll hear the entire range of an alto saxophone. The very highest octave is for advanced players only!

## Same note, different timbre

There are at least fourteen notes that can be played on all four saxophones: from the concert pitch A♭ below Middle C (A♭3), up to the next A (A4).

If you play these concert pitches on the four most popular saxophone voices, you'll hear — literally — four different voices, each with its own timbre or tone. The differences are considerable, and in most cases, you'll be able to identify a saxophone voice after hearing just a few notes.

TIPCODE

**Tipcode SAX-009**
In this Tipcode, the exact same phrase is played on a soprano, an alto, a tenor and a baritone. Listen to the different timbres.

# TRANSPOSING INSTRUMENTS

If you play the piano, and your chart shows a C, you play the
C key and you'll hear a C. If a saxophone chart shows a C, you
finger a C, but you will hear a different note. This is because
saxophones are *transposing instruments*.

### Concert instruments
Pianos, guitars, and many other instruments are called *concert
instruments*, because they sound in *concert pitch*: The note you
play is the note you hear. With transposing instruments, this is
different.

### E♭ instruments
If you finger a C on an alto or a baritone, for example, you will
hear an E♭ (E-flat). These two saxes are *E♭ instruments*.

### B♭ instruments
If you finger a C on a soprano or a tenor, you will hear a B♭ (B-
flat). These two saxes are *B♭ instruments*.

### Same fingerings
This may sound a little complicated at first, but it has one great
advantage: No matter which sax you're playing, you *always* use
the same fingerings. For example, a Middle C on paper always
means that you close the six pearl keys + key 7 (right little finger).
The note that comes out is the note the composer wanted to hear.

**TIPCODE**

**Tipcode SAX-010**
This Tipcode demonstrates the
different concert pitches for the
four most popular saxophone
voices.

27

The note C5 on paper, the corresponding fingering C for all saxes, and the resulting concert pitches.

Soprano   Alto   Tenor   Baritone

## Transposed parts

A saxophonist's part doesn't tell you which pitches to play, but which notes to finger: Saxophonists read transposed parts. When you play your part, your instrument 'transposes' the written note to the pitch the composer had in mind. If you're playing an alto and the composer wants to hear a concert E♭, you'll find a C in your part. If a tenor is supposed to sound an E♭, the part will show an F.

Again: The ranges of the four most popular saxophones. The lowest note on a soprano (B♭) sounds an A♭ on the piano; the lowest note on an alto (also B♭) sounds a D♭ on the piano, and so on.

C1   C2   C3   C4 (middle C)   C5   C6   C7   C8

Soprano B♭ – F♯

Alto B♭ – F♯

Tenor B♭ – F♯

Baritone A – F♯

### Saxophones in C
Wouldn't it be much easier if saxophones sounded in C, like pianos? Yes, but making a saxophone in another tuning would also change its timbre. A tenor saxophone in C, for example, would be smaller than the tenor in B♭. Due to this smaller size, its sound would tend toward that of an alto.

### Alto in C?
An alto couldn't be made to sound in C at all: It would have to be smaller than a soprano — or almost as big as a tenor… That said, saxophones in C and other tunings have been made (see pages 148–150), but the E♭ and B♭ instruments have outlasted them.

### Other wind instruments
Incidentally, saxes are not the only transposing instruments. Most trumpets and clarinets, for example, are in B♭, just like the soprano and tenor saxes; alto flutes are in G, and French horns in F and B♭.

29

# Learning to play

It doesn't take much time to learn to play the saxophone, but it takes quite a lot of time to learn how to play it well — to play it in tune, and to develop a good sound. A chapter about some of the main elements of learning the instrument, and about taking lessons, and practicing.

It's not the complicated-looking mechanism that takes so much time to learn. After all, it was devised to make playing the saxophone as easy as possible.

### Good sound

It will take you longer to make the instrument sound the way you want it to sound: A saxophone only sounds as good as the person who plays it. First of all, playing a wind instrument is more than blowing air through a tube. To sound good, you need a good breathing technique. Good air stream control is also important for being able to play in tune — and to play long phrases, of course.

### Embouchure

The second important element for your sound is how you use your lips, jaws, tongue, and all the muscles around them. Altogether that is known as the *embouchure*. This term is based on the French word for mouth, *bouche*.

## LESSONS

A good saxophone teacher covers everything that has to do with playing the instrument — from developing air stream control and embouchure to playing in tune, and from reading music to good posture.

### Locating a teacher

Looking for a private teacher? Larger music stores may have teachers on staff, or they can refer you to one, and some players have found great teachers in musicians they have seen in performance. The Internet is a great resource as well (see page 181). You can also consult your local Musicians' Union, the band director at a high school in your vicinity, or check the classified ads in newspapers, in music magazines or on supermarket bulletin boards. Professional private teachers will usually charge between twenty-five and fifty dollars per hour. Some make house calls, for which you'll pay extra.

> ### Group or individual lessons
> *Instead of taking individual lessons, you can also go for group lessons if that's an option in your area. Private lessons are more expensive, but can be tailored exactly to your needs.*

### Collectives

You also may want to check whether there are any teachers' collectives or community music schools in your vicinity. These organizations may offer extras such as ensemble playing, master classes, and clinics, in a wide variety of styles and at various levels.

### Questions, questions

On your first visit to a teacher, don't ask only how much it costs. Here are some other questions.

- Is a free **introductory lesson** included? This is a good way to find out how well you get on with the teacher, and, for that matter, with the instrument.

- Is the teacher interested in taking you on as a student if you are just doing it **for the fun of it**, or are you expected to practice at least three hours a day?

- Do you have to make a large investment in method books right away, or is **course material provided**?

- Can you **record your lessons**, so that you can listen at home to how you sound, and once more to what has been said?

- Are you allowed to fully concentrate on the **style of music** you want to play, or will you be required — or stimulated! — to learn other styles?

- Is this teacher going to make you **practice scales** for two years, or will you be pushed onto a stage as soon as possible?

- Many **more helpful tips** on choosing a teacher can be found in *Tipbook Music for Kids and Teens* (see page 221).

**33**

# PRACTICING

What goes for every instrument especially goes for wind instruments: It's better to practice half an hour every day than a couple of hours twice a week. This is especially true because of your embouchure. If you don't play for a few days, your embouchure will suffer straight away.

### Three times ten
If you find it hard to practice half an hour a day, try dividing it up into two quarter-hour sessions, or three of ten minutes each.

### The right pitch
On a saxophone, the notes you finger do not sound in pitch automatically: They can easily sound a bit *flat* (too low) or *sharp* (high). Therefore, you have to learn how to play the notes at the right pitch by using your embouchure and air stream control. The more you play, the faster you will learn to hear whether you are voicing them properly.

### Neighbors
If neighbors or housemates are bothered by your practice sessions, it can be enough to simply agree to fixed practice times. If you really play a lot, consider soundproofing a room — even a large cupboard can be big enough. There are books available on sound insulation, you can ask around to find people who sound-proofed a room, or you can hire a specialized contractor to do the job. As a much cheaper alternative, you may consider practicing someplace else: There may be rehearsal studios that you can rent by the hour in your area, for example.

### Mutes and towels
Most saxophone mutes (a padded ring — or an ordinary towel — that you insert into the bell) aren't very effective. They make the lowest notes difficult to play, while higher notes will hardly be dampened at all: Their toneholes are still wide open.

34

### Pack it up

A more effective alternative is a special bag that completely covers the instrument, considerably cutting down the volume. You play the horn using the three openings of the bag: one for each hand, and one for your mouthpiece.

### Case

A similar muffler consists of an ABS plastic case which reduces the sound of the instrument to an absolute minimum. A built-in microphone and a set of headphones allows you to hear what you play.

TIP

### Your own ears

*If you are playing in a loud band, or if you're practicing at full volume in a small space, consider using ear protection. Basic earplugs and earmuffs effectively cut down the volume, but playing in tune and working on your sound becomes really hard: This type of protection makes your instrument and the rest of the band sound as if they're next door. A better but more expensive solution is to use ear protectors that have (preferably adjustable or customized) filters.*

### Baby teeth and braces

The youngest saxophone players may be hindered when they start losing their baby teeth: If you don't have all your teeth, the instrument may wobble in your mouth. Usually braces aren't that much of a problem, although if you play for a particularly long time, a lower brace might start giving you some trouble.

### Play-along CDs

Playing with others is usually more fun than practicing alone — and you don't need to invite a band or an orchestra for that purpose: There are all kinds of CDs available to play along to, in all kinds of styles, for beginners as well as for advanced saxophonists. Your own part is left off, leaving the other musicians for you to play with.

### Computer lessons

If you have a computer handy, you can also use special CD-ROMs to practice with. Some feature entire orchestras: You can decide for yourself how fast you want a piece to be played, and which parts you want to hear. There is also software that allows you to slow down difficult phrases on CDs, so you can find out what's going on at your own tempo.

### Metronome

Most pieces of music are supposed to be played at a steady tempo. Practicing with a metronome helps you to do so. A *metronome* is a small mechanical or electronic device that ticks or bleeps out a steady adjustable pulse, so you can tell immediately if you're dragging or speeding.

*Two mechanical metronomes and two electronic ones.*

TIP

## Record your lessons

*If you record your saxophone lessons, you can listen to what was said, and especially to how you sounded when you get home. You can learn a lot by listening carefully to yourself playing. That's why many musicians record themselves when they are practicing too. All you need is a small recording device with a built-in microphone. Better equipment (a minidisc recorder with a separate microphone, for instance) is more expensive, but the recordings are usually more enjoyable to listen to.*

### Listen and play

And finally, visit festivals, concerts, and jam sessions. One of the best ways to learn to play is seeing other musicians at work. Living legends or local amateurs — every concert's a learning experience. And the best way to learn to play? Play a lot!

# 5

# Buying a sax

A saxophone is not the cheapest instrument to start off
with, due to its complicated keywork, for one thing. On the
other hand: the very best saxophones are quite affordable,
compared to other instruments. This chapter covers
everything you need to know before you get yourself a
saxophone, rented or purchased, new or secondhand.
How to go about selecting and play-testing an instrument is
covered in Chapter 6, A good sax.

A decent new alto sax easily costs between five or six hundred and a thousand dollars; for a decent tenor, expect to pay from some eight to fifteen hundred dollars. Why so much? Because making a decent sax is a time-consuming affair.

### Too cheap

Cheap saxophones, as great as they may look, are often harder to play in tune than good instruments. The keywork of cheap instruments tends to distort easily and may not allow for decent repairs; keywork of lesser quality also makes the instrument harder to play, especially for a beginner. Also, the body may dent easily. Teachers will generally advise you to stay away from the cheapest instruments and invest at least five or six hundred dollars for your first horn — and some will quote a higher minimum price.

### Professional

Professional altos typically start around three thousand dollars. The most expensive altos are about twice this price. Tenor prices are usually five to ten percent higher.

**TIP**

### Professional?

Tip: When it comes to musical instruments, the label 'professional' is often misused, and you will also find it on low-budget instruments that are very unlikely to be the choice of professional players.

### Sopranos

A soprano often costs a little more than an alto or a tenor of similar quality: Because of its small size, it's harder to make a soprano that plays both well and in tune.

### Baritones

Baritones do not come cheap due to their size and because fewer of them are made. Prices often start around three thousand dollars, going up to more than four times that amount.

### See and hear

To the casual viewer, professional saxes look just like budget models. To *see* the differences you'll need to take a close look. To *hear* the differences you have to be a pretty good player. In other words: You can enjoy playing a decent student saxophone for quite a few years.

### Time and effort

So why pay more? More expensive saxophones have more time and effort put into them, and higher quality materials are used; they have a better mechanism, stronger rods, better springs, and adjustable keys. Ornamental engravings and a silver or gold plating rather than a lacquer finish push up the price as well. Making these instruments often involves more handwork, as well as research and development.

### A better sound

As a result, a more expensive horn will usually sound better, and it's very likely to be more reliable and easier to play in tune, and to last and stay in adjustment longer than a budget instrument. Also, higher quality instruments generally have higher resale values.

### Maintenance, reeds...

In addition to the price you pay for the horn and a case or bag, you have to save some money for the required maintenance (see pages 141-142) and for reeds, of course. You can also invest in your instrument, for example by buying a better mouthpiece, or a new neck — which is worthwhile only if you and your instrument are good enough.

# THE SHOP

A saxophone is a precision instrument that needs to be properly maintained and adjusted. Even new saxophones usually need to be adjusted before they play well. That's why you're best off buying your instrument in a shop that has trained technicians on staff. Then you know that they know what they are doing, and that they probably won't send you home with an inferior, badly adjusted instrument.

### Check-up
Every saxophone needs periodic cleaning, oiling, and adjusting (*COA*). If you have bought a new instrument, that service may be free the first time.

### Another store
When you're going to buy an instrument, it can't do any harm to visit a few different stores. Every shop has its own sound, and you'll hear different stories and opinions depending on where you go. Also, not all shops stock the same brands.

### Time and space
The more saxes there are to choose from, the harder the choice can be — but the better your chances of finding the one you're looking for. Be sure to take your time, and remember that it's better to come back another time than to play an hour or more in a row. Some stores have separate rooms for play-testing, so that you don't bother the other customers — or vice versa.

### On approval
Some stores allow you to take an instrument on approval, so that you can assess it at your leisure, both at home and in rehearsals or performances.
This is more common with pro-level instruments than with cheap ones, and you are more likely to be offered this opportunity if you're a good player than if you are choosing your first saxophone.

### Different
An advantage of trying out a saxophone at home is that you are used to how your own instrument sounds there, which helps you to compare properly. In a store everything sounds different — even your own instrument.

TIP

> ### Not the same
> Even two 'identical' saxophones will never sound exactly the same. So always buy the instrument you think sounds best, and not an 'identical' one from the stockroom. The same goes for mouthpieces.

### Buying online

You can also buy saxophones online or by mail order. This makes it impossible to compare instruments, but most online and mail-order companies offer a return service for most or all of their products: If you're not happy with it, you can send it back within a certain period of time. Of course the instrument should be in new condition when you send it back. Tip: If you buy a really cheap instrument online, it may be hard to find a technician who wants to service it.

# RENTING

Rather than buying a saxophone, you can rent one. Expect to pay around twenty-five to fifty dollars a month for an alto. Usually, there's a minimum rental period – three months, for instance, or a school year. The rental fee is usually set as a percentage of the retail price of the instrument.

### Various plans

It is impossible to provide a detailed description of the infinite amount of different plans, terms, and conditions you will likely encounter when you decide to rent an instrument. But here are the basics:

- Many rental plans are actually **rent-to-own plans**: The instrument is yours once the periodic payments you've made equals the list price. Note that this list price will usually be higher than what you would have paid had you just bought

**43**

the instrument outright — which explains why most of these plans are interest free. The profit is in the difference between the discounted street price or going price, and the list price.

- Most of these rent-to-own or **hire-purchase plans** also have an option to buy the instrument before you're fully paid up; if you choose to buy the instrument, your rent paid to date will usually be applied to the instrument.

- With a **lease plan** — also known as a straight rental plan or **rent-to-rent plan** — you simply keep paying rent until you return the instrument. Rates are usually lower on these plans than those of rent-to-own plans. With these plans, renting for a long period of time will be, of course, more expensive than buying the instrument.

### Maintenance and insurance

Maintenance is usually included in the rental fee, but some plans offer it as a separate expense. The main thing is to make sure you don't have to worry about it. Insurance may be included as well. Make sure you understand what is and isn't covered under your lease or rental plan.

- Does the fee **include** instrument set-up, maintenance, and finance or bank charges?

- If **insurance** is included, does it also cover theft and loss?

- Do you get a **replacement instrument** if yours needs maintenance?

- Do you have to pay an **origination fee**, an application fee, or a deposit? These costs are usually non-refundable; they often may be applied to the rental, however.

- Is there a **reconditioning fee**, a stocking fee, or a depreciation fee when you return the instrument?

### Read

Always carefully read the contract before signing it. Some stores have contracts that are relatively long and hard to understand. Generally the less verbiage, the fewer loopholes for you to get caught in.

# SECONDHAND INSTRUMENTS

Are secondhand saxophones much cheaper? Not always. A decent used instrument can easily cost as much as a new student model — but you can get great used horns, made thirty, forty years ago or more, for less than a new saxophone of similar quality.

## Overhaul

Before a saxophone can be sold again, it often needs a partial or complete overhaul, which has its effect on the price of the horn. Still, a used modern instrument will be cheaper than the same one out of the box, of course.

## Vintage horns

Many jazz players prefer vintage saxophones, because they feel they sound richer, fatter, and warmer than instruments made in recent years. Some examples of vintage or classic horns are mentioned in Chapter 14, *Brands*. If you're looking for one, it's good to know that there are specialized vintage saxophone stores.

## For beginners?

There are also great vintage horns for less money. Note, however, that not every old horn is a good one, and that old horns may be harder to play than new ones. There's more about this on pages 79–81.

## Privately or in a store

Secondhand saxophones are sold through music stores, and they're offered for sale in the classified sections in newspapers, on bulletin boards in stores, and on the Internet.
Purchasing a used instrument from a private party may be cheaper than buying the same one from a store. One of the advantages of buying a used instrument from a retailer, however, is that you can go back if you have questions or problems. Chances are the instrument has been checked and adjusted before being sold to you, and the store may offer you a limited warranty to back its dependability. Also, you may be able to

45

choose between a number of models in stock, and in some cases you can even exchange the instrument you bought for a different one within a certain period of time.

### Competitive price
A good dealer will sell at a competitive price, whereas private sellers might ask way too much — either because they don't know any better, or because they think that you don't.

### Take someone along
If you go to buy a pre-owned saxophone, it's even more important to take along an advanced player who knows about the instrument — especially if you're going to buy privately. Otherwise you might turn down a decent sax just because it doesn't look good, or get saddled with an instrument that looks

*The differences: left, an alto built by the inventor, Adolphe Sax, from 1864.*

*Right, a modern alto: more keys, and a bit larger.*

TIP

### Sieve
*Many decent saxes in disrepair can be made to sound good, even if they leak like a sieve and you can barely get a sound out of them. If you buy an instrument like this, you should be aware that it can easily cost you hundreds of dollars to get it fixed.*

great but doesn't sound good or play in tune. Technical tips on buying secondhand instruments can be found on pages 75–78.

### Appraisal
If you want to be sure you're not paying too much, get the instrument appraised first. An expert technician or salesperson can tell you what it's worth, whether it needs any work done, and what that's going to cost you. If the seller is unwilling to allow this, that could be a warning sign of serious problems.

## AND FINALLY...
The most beautiful sax sound is often that of your favorite sax player. So should you buy the same horn? Not necessarily. Even if you play exactly the same sax, mouthpiece, and reed, you'll still sound different.

### Who's blowing the horn
Have one saxophonist play a couple of different saxes, and you will hear pretty much the same sound each time. Have two players play the same sax, and they will sound as different as they always do. In other words: The sound depends more on the player than on the instrument.

### More to read
If you want to be really well-informed before you go out to buy or rent an instrument, do visit the major saxophone websites

47

online, and get hold of as many saxophone brochures, catalogs, and pricelists as you can find. Also check out musicians' magazines that do product reviews of the instrument, and do read other books on the saxophone. Most of these additional resources are listed on pages 178–179 of this book.

### Fairs and conventions

One last tip: If a music trade show or convention is being held in your area, check it out. Besides lots of instruments you can try out and compare, you will come across plenty of product specialists, as well as numerous fellow sax players who are always a good source of information and inspiration.

# 6

# A good sax

*At first glance, all alto saxophones look alike. And all tenors too. Yet they'll feel different when you play them, and they will sound different, and some have extra keys or other special features. This chapter tells you about those differences, and offers tips for play-testing saxophones and evaluating their sound.*

The mouthpiece and the reed are of major influence on how a sax plays and sounds. Both are discussed separately in Chapters 7 and 8.

### This chapter

Why two 'identical' saxes can sound and play so differently is linked to all kinds of things. This chapter begins with the instrument's finish and body. The next main subjects discussed are the neck (page 55), the key system (page 59), ergonomics (63), springs and adjustment (65), the pads (67), and secondhand and vintage instruments (75).

TIP

---

**Your ears**

*If you prefer to select a sax using your ears alone, then go straight to the tips for auditioning and play-testing the instrument, which begin on page 69.*

---

### Various experts

Sax players rarely agree about anything. The following chapters won't tell you who is right, or what is best, but rather what various experts think about different issues. You'll discover whom you agree with only by playing and by listening — to saxophones, and to saxophonists.

### Prices

The price indications mentioned in this chapter refer to altos and tenors, unless specified otherwise.

# THE FINISH

Nearly all saxes are made of brass. However, they belong to the family of woodwind instruments, just like the clarinet, the oboe, and other instruments (see Chapter 12). As unfinished brass stains easily and makes your hands smell, most saxophones are finished in one way or another. Apart from the cosmetic aspect, the finish may also have a — very slight — effect on the instrument's sound.

### Lacquer
Most saxophones are finished with a glossy, transparent lacquer, which often has a shade of gold (*gold lacquer*).

### Silver
Silver-plated instruments are usually said to sound a bit brighter: The silver plating is thinner than lacquer, so it has less of a muffling effect. Some brands offer instruments both in lacquered and silver-plated versions, the latter easily costing two to six hundred dollars more.

### Gold
Gold-plated saxes are rare. They're often said to sound slightly warmer than silver-plated instruments. Gold plating is more expensive than silver plating, and it's quite vulnerable, gold being so soft.

### Nickel
Nickel-plated saxes were commonly built well into the 1960s. Some student instruments still have nickel-plated keys, as nickel is relatively inexpensive and durable, and requires little maintenance. Its main drawback is that many people are allergic to it.

### Colored saxophones
A few companies sell colored saxophones with a choice of colors and designs, or featuring more durable black nickel plating. A colored finish may cost you an extra three to six hundred dollars.

### Matte and unfinished
At the other end of the spectrum there are instruments with a matte finish (often referred to as *hand-brushed*), and there are even unfinished horns.

51

## More than one

*Many instruments feature more than one finish: silver-plated keys and a lacquered body, for example, or glossy keys on a matte body.*

### Engravings

Many saxes have a design, the brand name, and the series name engraved on the bell, and some have engravings elsewhere too. A few brands offer non-engraved horns as an option. Engravings can be made by hand, or using a laser.

*Saxophone engraving on the bell (Yamaha).*

## THE BODY

When it comes to sound, the instrument's exact dimensions are far more important than its finish. The material the body is made of plays a role too.

### Brass

Most saxophones are made of *yellow brass*. Some instruments have a distinctive red shade, as they're made of brass with a higher copper content (c. 85%, rather than c. 70%). While some say that this makes the instrument sound brighter, others hear a warmer timbre.

### Solid silver or gold

Similarly, a solid silver body is usually said to produce extra brightness, clarity, and projection or 'carrying power,' while other saxophone experts and players claim the opposite. These varying opinions have as much to do with how people experience sound as with the words they choose to describe it. Solid gold saxophones — rare as they are — are typically said to have a 'rich', warm, round, and homogenous sound.

### The bore

When you play, the air column inside the saxophone vibrates. It's only logical that the exact shape of that column (the *bore*, *i.e.*, the internal dimensions of the body) has a lot of influence on the timbre of the instrument. For example, vintage instruments are said to sound the way they do partially because of a narrower bore. The smaller bore also increases their blowing resistance.

### Hard to tell

Other than that, it's nearly impossible to compare saxophones by examining the dimensions of their bores: Being conical (*i.e.*, widening) all the way, differences are hard to tell or to measure. This explains why so much less is written and known about this specific feature than about alloys, finishes, and other factors that are often less decisive for the instrument's sound.

### Curved or straight sopranos

Traditionally, soprano saxophones have a straight body, but some brands offer curved models too. Curved sopranos are often said to have a milder, fuller sound, which is closer to the timbre of the other saxophones than the sound of a straight soprano.

53

## Curved or straight necks

Many straight sopranos, especially in the higher price range, come with both a curved and a straight neck. The words used to describe the difference in sounds produced by curved and straight necks are often similar to the ones mentioned above: Curved necks are usually said to promote a darker, fuller, warmer, milder tone. Conversely, sopranos with straight necks are typically believed to sound brighter and edgier.

*A straight soprano with a straight neck, one with a curved neck, and a curved soprano.*

### Less tiresome

A different consideration is that a soprano with a curved neck is a bit less tiresome to play: To have your mouthpiece at the required angle, a straight soprano with a straight neck should be held close to horizontal. The curved soprano, in that respect, is the more comfortable horn to play, and it 'feels' most like the other saxophones.

### Two more

Two more thoughts? Some players think that straight sopranos often have better *intonation* than curved models, meaning that they're usually easier to play in tune — but note that sopranos are always harder to play in tune than larger saxes. One of the reasons some saxophonists prefer curved horns is that you can hear yourself better when you play, as the bell doesn't point away from your ears.

### Straight altos and tenors

A few brands make straight altos and tenors. Most of what has been said above applies to these instruments as well.

*A straight alto sax.*

# THE NECK

The closer a part is to your mouth, the larger its influence on the way you play and sound. This is what makes mouthpieces and reeds so important, and the same goes for necks or — in the UK — *crooks*.

### Two or three

Some saxophones come with two or even three different necks, each neck sporting a different bore, a different finish, or both. If two necks are supplied, one neck usually has a mellower tone, while the other sounds a bit brighter. Swapping necks can help you to adapt your sound to the acoustics of the venue you're playing (a 'hard' room requiring a mellower tone, for instance), to the style of music, or your role in the group (playing lead or section, for example).

### Finish and bore

As necks are so important, their finish may affect your tone more than the finish elsewhere on the instrument. Some examples: Black-nickeled necks are said to offer the brightest sound, followed by silver-plated, lacquered, and unfinished necks. Remember, however, that the bore and construction of the neck will be more important than its finish or material.

### Much to improve

While most horns perform well with the neck they're sold with, you may be able to improve an instrument by providing it with another one. A better neck can enhance almost every aspect of the horn, from timbre and response to intonation.

### Prices

An intermediate saxophone may already benefit from a two-hundred-dollar neck, and if your sax is good enough, you may want to spend a lot more on a seamless solid sterling silver neck, for example. If you want to try something really different, you can also go for a wooden neck.

### Expert required

Necks and saxophones do not always match. The end of the neck, the *tenon*, should of course fit the body's neck receiver — but that's not all. For example, the neck octave vent should be in the right place relative to the rest of the instrument, to prevent intonation problems. In other words: Choosing another neck usually requires consulting a saxophone expert. One more tip: Another neck may require another mouthpiece. The two are closely interrelated, just like mouthpieces and reeds.

### Reinforced necks

Reinforced (tenor) necks are available, and they can be custommade too. Generally speaking, the added mass will make for a less resonant but more focused, tighter sound.

## TONEHOLES, POSTS, AND THE BELL

The more you look at saxophones, the easier it'll be to spot differences in the way they're made. Comparing a very expensive horn to the cheapest one in the store will help you to learn to appreciate these differences. Check, for example, the key guards and the way they're attached; have a look at the *bell brace* (the connection between the bell and the body), and compare other details. Often, student instruments have less delicate parts than pro horns. As a result, they may look like

A bell brace.

57

they're sturdier, while in reality pro horns will usually outlast cheaper models.

### Tonehole edges
Run your finger along the edges of the toneholes. The smoother and thicker they are, the less they will cut into the pads, reducing the chance of leaks. The tonehole edges should be level as well, but that is hard to check.

### Rolled toneholes
Very few brands still make saxes with rolled tonehole edges. Rolled toneholes are very pad-friendly, offering added protection against leaks. They also help reduce noise (key action is quieter!) and make for a slightly softer feel.

*Regular (above) and rolled (below) toneholes (Keilwerth).*

### Posts
The posts that hold the key system in place are soldered onto the body either individually (*post construction*), or in groups, by means of metal strips. This so-called *rib construction* or *ribbed construction* is more common.

### Ribs
A ribbed construction helps make for a sturdier body, but the ribs may also constrict the horn's sound and resonance a bit. Some makers counteract this effect by reducing the size and weight of the ribs; others claim the ribs promote a warmer

**58**

overall sound... *Tip:* Some companies produce instruments featuring a partial ribbed construction.

rib

### Detachable bell
Another detail: Many saxophones feature a detachable bell, and on some the bow can be removed too. This offers easy access for removing dents, for instance.

# THE KEY SYSTEM

Over the years, the key system has undergone lots of improvements. Modern saxophones are easier to play, key shapes have been adapted for a more comfortable feel, extra keys have been added while others disappeared, and adjustable side and palm keys have been introduced.

### Nineteen
The very first saxes had nineteen keys. More and more were added, as the illustration on page 46 shows. Other keys disappeared over the years. Most modern saxes have twenty-four or twenty-five keys, the extra one being the high F♯.

### High F♯
The *high F♯ key* makes playing this high note a little easier. This key, introduced in the 1960s, has become a standard item

on almost all saxophones, and some companies offer
it as an option. The high F♯ key is also featured on many of
the popular replicas of pre-1960 horns, which originally came
without this key.

*The high F♯ key.
The tonehole is
located higher
up (see below).*

High F♯ key (C5) ―

### High F♯, no key

Some saxophonists prefer horns without the high F♯ key, as
they feel it affects the instrument's timbre and resonance.
Besides, most good players can play this note without the extra
key. The same goes for high G, a note for which some soprano
saxes have an extra key.

*A sax without
(left), and
one with a high
F♯ (right).*

High F♯ key cu▸

## Low A

An extra key found on most modern baritones is *low A*. To produce this note, low A *baritones* are slightly longer than the traditional baris. Note that 'low A' only refers to the horn's lowest note, and not to its tuning: Low A baritones are still E♭ instruments!

### Automatic octave key

Occasionally, catalogs promote saxophones by extolling their *automatic octave key*. Sounds impressive, but this has been a standard item since the 1930s. When you press the octave key, the mechanism 'automatically' determines which of the two octave vents should be opened. The lower octave vent opens for the lower notes of the upper register (D through G♯). On higher notes the upper octave vent opens, and the first one closes automatically. Before, saxes had a separate key for each octave vent.

### Automatic G♯

The *automatic G♯* or *articulated G♯*, introduced on expensive instruments in the 1930s, has also become pretty much a standard feature. It opens the G♯ key when you are using the low G♯, B, or B♭ key (left little finger), making it easier to alternate between any of these notes and G♯. However, the system has one drawback: Your little finger has to work harder because it has to operate so many keys simultaneously. That's why some saxes have the option of disengaging it.

### Non-sticking G♯

The G♯ key cup tends to stick rather easily. To make sure it opens every time it needs to, saxophones have features with names like 'G♯ Pad Cup Lifting Mechanism' or 'Spring-Controlled G♯.'

### Articulated C♯

If you play a low B or low B♭, your left little finger can easily get hung up on the C♯ key. The result? C♯, instead of the intended notes. Most saxes therefore have a small rod that closes the C♯ key as soon as you use the low B or B♭ key. This *articulated* C# ensures that you get the note you want.

### Tilting keys
Most professional and some of the more affordable saxes feature *tilting little finger keys*. When you play the C# key, for example, the B♭ key tilts toward it, making shifts between these notes a lot easier. This is especially useful for certain technical passages.

### Additional keys
Occasionally, saxophones have other special keys. For example, there are saxophones with an extra key that operates a second vent hole on the neck, making the high harmonics easier to play. Other extra keys are 'automatic,' such as special keys that correct the pitch of certain notes by closing or opening one or more vents.

TIP

### Lingo
Most of the features that may help you select an instrument have been included on these pages. However, when reading saxophone websites and catalogs, you're bound to come across many more technical terms and other saxophone lingo, such as floating or rocker-type mechanisms. Usually, these terms do not refer to things that might influence the way the instrument plays or sounds in any significant way.

### Power-forged keys
Sometimes you find saxophones advertised as having *power-forged keys* — but this is a standard item on pretty much every sax: It means the keys are shaped by pressure, when the metal is cold, rather than cast.

### Double key arms
To enhance their stability and help prevent damage and misaligned keys, some manufacturers use double key arms for the pad cups of the large bell keys (low C and lower).

# ERGONOMICS

Every alto sax is the same size. All tenors are the same size too — and so on. However, it is likely that one make or series suits you better than another. Even the exact location of the hanger loop may be of influence, for example.

### Sit down
Though standing up is often considered the best way to play a wind instrument, as this position gives you better air stream control, many musicians play sitting down — so try out a horn that way too.

### Side and palm keys
Check the position of the side and palm keys. If they sit high, and you have small hands, you may find them difficult to reach, or you may open them accidentally. A compact design may be easier to play — even if you have bigger hands.

### Oversized and contoured
Another way to improve fingering ease and the playing comfort of the instrument is to use oversized keys and levers, for instance for high F♯ and the side F♯ key, or sculptured

*Sax with a spatula key for the front F.*

Front F

TIPBOOK SAXOPHONE

(contoured, concave, finger fitting...) spatula keys, pearls, or palm keys.

### Another style

Some companies do a lot of design research themselves; others rely on well-established designs. *French style keys*, for instance, are keys that are modeled after a design of the French Selmer saxophones. When trying out saxophones, some models may feel kind of weird at first, due to differently shaped keys — but you get used to another key design pretty quickly.

### Adjustable keys

To make the instrument fit your hands and your style of playing, most better saxophones come with a number of adjustable keys — either as a standard feature, or as an option. Examples are G♯, high F, E, D, and some of the little finger and palm keys.

*Adjustable keys*

adjustment nuts

### Risers and extensions

Alternatively, a saxophone technician can adjust your instrument to your liking by reshaping keys or by replacing some of the bumpers with thinner or thicker ones. Should the side or palm keys be too low, a set of *key risers* can make them more accessible. These risers can easily be self-installed. For other keys, various types of key extensions are available, and some keys can be built up with cork or epoxy, for example.

### Adjustable thumb hooks
Most thumb hooks can be adjusted both sideways and up and down. If not the case with your instrument, you can usually have its thumb hook replaced by an adjustable one.

### Plastic or metal
Thumb hooks come in plastic and metal. Some players find the plastic ones more comfortable, and plastic hooks can't discolor or cause skin rash. If a metal hook bothers you, you can slide a soft (imitation) rubber *thumb saver* over it.

### Thumb hooks and sound
Conversely, some sensitive players replace their thumb hooks by special metal versions that are claimed to improve the sound of the horn, enhancing its resonance and helping to produce a bigger and more brilliant sound. Sound-enhancing metal replacement thumb rests are also available.

Thumb hook

Adjusting screw

Adjustable thumb hook.

## SPRINGS AND ADJUSTMENT

When play-testing saxophones, you'll notice that some instruments play easier or faster than others — each horn has a different *action*, to use the lingo. A horn's action depends on the quality of the keywork, and its adjustment.

### Heavy or light
On a well-adjusted instrument, the springs are set to give all

65

keys the same resistance. If the springs are adjusted too lightly, you may find that you can't really feel what you're doing, or that the keys become sluggish and don't return as quickly as they should. Keys that require too much pressure make you work too hard and slow you down.

### Key height
Key height should be properly adjusted as well. Key cups that open too far will slow you down and affect intonation for the worse (see pages 70–71). Adjusting action and key heights are jobs for a specialized technician.

### Sticking and bouncing
The keys should return quickly and smoothly to their resting positions when you release them: They're not supposed to stick, bounce, or rattle. You can test this by lightly depressing each and every key cup, and quickly sliding your finger off it sideways. Clattering keys can be caused by faulty adjustment too, and on used instruments missing felts or corks may be the culprit. Sticking keys can also be caused by sticky pads (see page 138).

*Corks and springs.*

Spring

Cork

### Springs

Most saxophones come with standard steel needle springs. Their blue or black hue is caused by a tempering treatment that gives the springs their required elasticity. The springs for the larger closed key cups (low C♯ and D♯) should be strong enough to make the pads seal the toneholes.

# PADS

The majority of saxophones have leather pads, consisting of a felt disc covered with a thin layer of sheep, goat, or baby goat (kid) leather. To seal the toneholes properly, the pads must be exactly centered over the holes. You can check this by looking at the impression of the tonehole's edge in the pad.

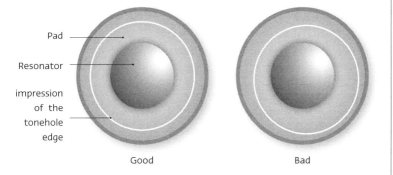

Pad

Resonator

impression
of the
tonehole
edge

Good                Bad

*The impression of the tonehole edge must be exactly in the middle of the pad.*

### Resonators

Resonators, the small discs in the middle of each pad, make the instrument sound a bit more direct and responsive, enhancing its brightness, cutting power, and projection. That's why some call them *tone boosters*. To mellow down an overly bright horn, you may consider using plastic resonators rather than the regular metal ones. Pads without resonators will make most saxophones sound lifeless and dull.

### Why leather?

Even though most players still prefer them, the traditional

67

leather pads have quite a few disadvantages: They require a lot of maintenance, and even then they don't last, mainly due to the fact that leather doesn't like to get wet and dry out repeatedly.

### Kangaroo

A growing number of saxophones have kangaroo leather pads. Kangaroo leather is very strong and lightweight, and it is claimed that kangaroo leather pads don't stick and that they produce less noise than regular leather pads.

### Non-leather pads

Non-leather pads, made of synthetic materials or rubber compounds, are insensitive to changes in humidity and easily outlast leather pads. Over the years they have been continuously improved, and their acceptance has grown accordingly.

### (Dis)advantages

Synthetic pads are often said to improve sealing and thus enhance resonance and response; they don't stick the way leather pads do; and they require less maintenance. On the other hand, they're usually more expensive than leather ones; they often require the toneholes of the instrument to be perfectly leveled; and some players just don't like the way they make their horn sound, play, or both.

### Faster

Some synthetic pad designs even allow for replacing the traditional key cups on the lowest toneholes by lightweight

**TIP**

### Pop

Pads that properly seal their toneholes make a resonant, 'pop'-like sound when closing the relevant key. However, a series of solid pops does not guarantee that a horn is leak-free. See page 78 for tips on how to locate leaks.

metal discs with built-in pads. The resulting weight reduction means that less spring tension is needed, which adds up to an even faster action.

# PLAY-TESTING

To judge the sound and intonation of a saxophone, you need to be able to play pretty well. If you don't (yet...), take a good saxophonist with you to try out the tips and tricks on the following pages, or go to a store that employs one.

### Somebody else
If someone else plays a couple of instruments for you, they'll never sound the same as if you were to play them yourself — but you will be able to hear the differences between the instruments. A tip: Even if you do play yourself, ask somebody else to play for you just to hear how the various horns sound from a distance. You'll find that you hear things you didn't hear before. Alternatively, you can point the instruments at a wall when you play, so that their sound is reflected back to you. This also helps when checking their intonation.

### The mouthpiece
To play-test horns, always use one mouthpiece (preferably your own) and reed. If not, you'll be comparing mouthpieces as much as saxophones. Ultimately, however, the saxophone of your choice may perform better with another mouthpiece and reed combination.

### Two tests in advance
There are two tests that allow you to quickly find out if a sax plays well enough to judge it.

• Play the instrument using **as little air pressure** as possible, and press the keys as lightly as you can. If you need to blow harder or squeeze the keys to get a note out, something is probably wrong.

69

- Play a B, pressing key 1 with your left index finger. Then go **down the scale**, softly, note by note, until you reach low B♭. The lowest notes are the trickiest ones. If the sax is leaking even a tiny bit, you'll have trouble getting them to speak.

# IN TUNE

On a saxophone you need to use your embouchure and air stream control to determine the exact pitch of the notes you play. This takes some time to learn, but you simply have to: A saxophone is never perfectly in tune by itself.

### Why not?
Why not? A saxophone could only be made to play every note perfectly in tune if it had an octave vent for each note — and there's just no room for that. Also, the positions of all toneholes are interrelated, which makes it impossible to make them all perfectly right. For example, high C♯ always sounds a bit sharp. This can be corrected by enlarging one or more toneholes, or by moving them down the tube just a bit — but that would make other notes sound flat.

### Better intonation
The better in tune the sax is to begin with, the less you'll need to adjust the notes. In other words, the better a saxophone's intonation, the easier it will be to play in tune.

### Smaller is harder
The smaller the instrument, the more critical the placement and the exact size of the toneholes are: A thousandth of an inch has more effect on a soprano than on a baritone. That's why sopranos are harder to make (and play) in tune than larger horns.

### Tuning, leaks, and key openings
The intonation of a sax can be judged only if it has been tuned (see page 119), if key heights have been properly adjusted

(key openings that are too large will make notes flat, and vice versa), and if there are no leaking pads.
*Tip:* A chromatic electronic tuner may be very helpful for the following tests. (There's more on tuners on pages 121–122.)

### Open C♯

One test is to go from open C♯ (no keys depressed) to the D above that note. This C♯ is always a bit flat, while low D is often a tad sharp.

### Larger intervals

Also play larger intervals, such as fifths (C–G, D–A, and so on) and octaves (C–C, D–D; *i.e.*, notes with and without the octave key) and check whether they sound in tune with one another — or rather, how easily you can play them in tune. For example, open C♯ being a little flat, and high C♯ a bit sharp, you will always have to adjust those pitches with your embouchure.

TIP

### Harmonic series

*For advanced players only: You can play a whole range of notes without moving from one fingering position, but using your air stream and embouchure only. You are then playing the harmonic series or the harmonics of the note you're fingering. When you finger low B♭, the first harmonic is the B♭ an octave higher, the second is the F above that, then the next B♭ and the D follow, and so on. These harmonics should be in tune with one another.*

### Best buy

The less in tune a sax plays, the better you have to play to make it sound acceptable. That's why beginners are better off buying a sax that plays in tune easily, rather than one that sounds great but has poor intonation. Horns that do both well are usually more expensive...

71

# LISTENING TIPS

Comparing instruments' sounds or timbres isn't easy — but the more often you do it, the more you'll hear. And the better you can play, the better you'll be able to appreciate the subtle timbre differences between horns. Here are some tips that can be helpful, followed by some remarks on what to listen for.

### Briefly at first
To make an initial selection of horns that you like, play them only briefly. Play something simple, otherwise you'll be concentrating more on playing than on listening. Scales, for instance, nice and slowly. If there's one sax that stands out from the rest at this stage, that'll often be the one you end up buying.

### Two by two
Once you've found a number of instruments that you really like, compare them two by two or three by three. Choose the best one and replace the one you like least with another horn. Again choose the best one, and so on.

### A little longer
In order to choose the very best horn from the two or three that remain, you may want to play each one a little longer so that you get to know them better. A tip: Even after just fifteen minutes of playing it gets harder to hear the differences. Take a break, or come back a day or two later.

### With your ears alone
Also try listening to these horns without looking to see which one you're playing: Use your ears only, without being influenced by prices, brand names, looks, or anything else. If the one that sounds best and plays best turns out to be the cheapest one, that's a bonus. Unless you particularly wanted a more expensive one, of course...

### Sheet music
If you don't know any music by heart, take sheet music with

you when you go to choose a new horn. The better you know a piece, the less you will be thinking about the notes, and the better you can concentrate on the instrument.

---

### No idea

If you have no idea where to start when you walk into a store, ask for two horns with distinctively different timbres — one with a notably dark tone and another that sounds particularly bright, for example. Decide what you like best and go on from there. Another tip: Play both the cheapest and the most expensive instrument available. Knowing the extremes can often help you to determine where you want to go.

---

### Your own horn

If you already own a saxophone, take it with you when you go out to buy a new one. That makes it easier to hear just how different instruments sound. On the other hand: You may be so used to your own instrument that it may seem to sound better or more in tune than other horns — even compared to more expensive ones.

### Different words

When two people listen to the same saxophone, they often use very different words to describe what they hear. What one considers shrill and thin (and so not attractive), another may consider bright or brilliant (and so not unattractive). And what one describes as dark and velvety, another may think dull or stuffy. Similarly, what one finds dark, another may find bright... It all depends on what you like, and on the words you use to describe it.

### Character

What sounds good and what doesn't also depends on the kind of music you play. If you play classical music, you're probably looking for a more controlled and intimate sound than if you

73

play jazz. And jazz players may want a more expressive sound, while Latin musicians may look for something brighter and more focused. Some saxophones allow you to play different styles and produce a wide range of tonal colors easier than other, less versatile instruments.

### Loud and soft
To judge the instruments, play them both loudly and softly throughout their entire range, and do so while playing each note separately, as well as joined together (*legato*).

### Low and high
Low notes should sound big and fat, even at low volumes. The highest notes should sound bright and clear, without getting too shrill or edgy, even when playing them loud.

### Tight and quick
When playing very loud, you should still be able to produce a focused, tight sound, without any notes breaking up — unless you want them to. Also play as softly as you can, and listen to hear if every note, from high to low, responds quickly and easily.

### A gradual change
Every horn sounds bigger, fuller, or fatter in its low register. In the high register, the tone will be thinner and tighter. When you play the instrument from low to high, that change should occur gradually. A critical spot is the jump between registers, from open C♯ (C5) to D (D5) — a half-step that involves closing a large number of keys.

### Your sound
As a final note: Saxophonists differ in sound much more than saxophones do. The saxophone that 'sounds best' to you, is probably the instrument that does most justice to your sound, and that allows your sound to come out easily.

74

### Preferences

Some players do prefer horns that have quite a big contrast
between the higher and lower ranges; others — mainly
classical players — prefer a more even-sounding instrument.

# SECONDHAND INSTRUMENTS

If you're thinking of purchasing a used instrument, there are
a few additional things you need to pay attention to. Number
one: It's always advisable to have an expert appraise a used
horn before you decide to buy it. A few special tips on buying
vintage or classic instruments can be found at the end of this
chapter.

### The lacquer

The lacquer may have started to wear off, and on old horns
there are various spots where it may have disappeared
completely — especially where the instrument rubs against
the player's hands and clothes. You may not like the looks, but
worn-off lacquer will not influence the sound to any noticeable
degree.

### Newly lacquered

Older saxes sporting a shiny lacquer finish all over the
instrument haven't been played very much, or they've been
relacquered. Relacquering involves removing the original
lacquer, a process which usually takes away some of the body's
metal as well. The latter will influence the instrument's sound,
and it may also result in an ill-fitting, wobbling key system. If
too much lacquer has been applied to the horn, the sound will
be muffled. This doesn't mean, however, that every relacquered
sax is a bad one.

### Silver or nickel, gold or lacquer

It's not hard to spot the difference between (expensive) silver-
plated or (inexpensive) nickel-plated horns: Nickel chips and

75

turns grayish, while silver wears down gradually and turns blue or black where polishing cloths can't reach it. Spotting the difference between gold-lacquered and (rare) gold-plated horns often requires a specialist's eye.

### Dents

Check the body, bell, and neck for dents. The further down the instrument, the less effect a dent will have. Conversely, even a tiny dent in the neck can impair a horn's intonation and timbre. Dents in the body can dislocate the key system, hindering the movement of certain keys. They can also alter the rigidity of the body, which may influence the tone.

### Where?

Besides the severity of the dents, their exact location will also affect the cost of their removal (a removable bell helps; see page 59). Used horns can also suffer from cracks or split soldering seams, but finding them usually requires an expert.

### The neck

Check the neck's shape too, especially when you're looking at a tenor or a baritone. These instruments may suffer from necks that have been bent down a little: Many players inadvertently exert a downward pressure on the neck when putting on the mouthpiece. This may result in one or more poorly responding notes, among other problems.

### The right neck

Of course, the neck should fit the saxophone in every sense (see page 56). Note that a different finish doesn't always mean that the neck doesn't belong to the instrument (see page 52).

### Rods and keys

Carefully check the key system. Worn-out key pearls can be easily replaced. If the instrument has a feather-light action, chances are that the springs need to be adjusted or replaced. A very light action may also be the result of excessive wear, so try the keywork for play: Rods should not be able to move back and forth or sideways, and keys and key cups should only move up and down. Check the rollers between the little finger keys as well; they should only roll and not move sideways.

### Play?

Play may cause leaks, as the key system will fail to properly seal the toneholes. Play also slows down the action; it's a source of squeaks and rattles, and it always gets worse.

TIPCODE

**Tipcode SAX-011**
This Tipcode shows you how to — carefully! — check keys for play.

### Bent rods

Check the rods to see if they're straight. Bent rods obstruct the action. The larger the horn, the longer its rods, the more vulnerable it is. Larger horns are more susceptible to dents too, because of their size.

### Rust and solder

Look for rust at the ends of rods and on screws. Rusty parts can drastically slow down the mechanism. Globs of solder can be a sign that the instrument has been sloppily repaired. This doesn't necessarily indicate an ineffective repair, but it does reduce the instrument's value.

### A snug fit

To make the mouthpiece fit snugly, the *neck cork* shouldn't be overcompressed or falling apart. If it is, you can't play-test the instrument unless you fix it temporarily with thread or paper (see page 122). The neck cork can easily be replaced. Also check to see that the neck tenon easily fits its receiver, and that there's no play in the joint. If there is, air will escape, affecting both intonation and response.

77

### Leaking pads

The pads should be smooth and soft. Locating a leaking pad is not as simple as it may seem. If, for instance, the low C doesn't respond well, it doesn't necessarily follow that the C key is the culprit — the leak could occur at a higher pad too. Slide a piece of paper under the suspect pads, and close them gently with the relevant keys. (For closed keys, rely on the spring to keep them closed.) If you don't feel any resistance when pulling the paper away, you've probably found your leak.

### Leak light

Sax technicians check for leaks with a special *leak light* that is inserted in the instrument. Where light leaks out, air will too. A bent neck or a leaking neck/body connection may also be the culprit.

### Too high, too low

Today most bands and orchestras tune to A=440 (see pages 119–121), and saxophones are designed to play at that pitch. You may find older horns, however, that were built to be tuned slightly higher or lower. You can learn how to play on such an instrument, but you won't be able to play it in a band that tunes to A=440. (You may be able to tune to that pitch, but by then your mouthpiece will be so far in or out that the intonation of your instrument will be off completely; again, see pages 119–121) Another disadvantage is that you'll have to adjust both your intonation and your hearing when you change to a modern horn later on.

### HP, LP

Saxes with a higher standard tuning can be identified by the abbreviation HP (high pitch) or by the indication A=451 or A=902, for example. Horns with a lower tuning have a number below 440 or 880, and they're often marked LP (low pitch). These indications are usually located near the serial number, below the thumb hook or on the bell. You can also tell an instrument with a deviant pitch by its length: HP instruments are about an inch shorter than saxes with standard tuning; low-pitched ones are about an inch taller.

TIP

> ## Smell
> If you go out to try an older used sax and a terrible smell comes wafting out of the case, you are looking at a poorly-maintained instrument, or at an instrument that hasn't been used in a long, long time. Don't worry: If the instrument is worth it, it can be completely restored (see page 142).

# VINTAGE SAXOPHONES

Many professional jazz players prefer classic or vintage saxophones, which are often said to sound darker and fatter than today's horns, and to offer a bigger dynamic range. Some examples are listed in Chapter 14, *Brands*.

### Not all the same
Not every vintage sax is a good one. For one thing, when horns were still made by hand, the differences between 'identical' instruments were greater than they are today. One vintage horn of a reputable type and year, therefore, may not be as good as the other.

### A good player
Saxophonists who favor vintage horns often love their tonal range, and the fact that they can color the timbre to a large extent. Of course you need to be able to truly play the instrument if you want to harness and control its flexibility, and to play the horn in tune: Most vintage instruments are not known for their great intonation. Also, they require a better air stream control and breath support.

### Heavier action
In the old days, much less was done to create ergonomic designs. One example? Today's octave key, shaped in a sort of crescent around the thumb rest, is a lot easier to play than the old-fashioned button key. Old altos are less of a problem than

79

vintage tenors or baris, as their keys are slightly closer together and you're moving less metal.

*A round octave key on a 1927 Buescher Truetone.*

Octave key

Thumb rest (left thumb)

Octave key

Thumb rest (left thumb)

*A modern octave key. The palm keys are also different.*

## Special keys

*Old saxes may have keys that new ones don't. An example is the G♯ trill key, designed to play trills between G and G♯ with your right middle finger. It was used on certain German and American saxes made before 1940, as was a special key to trill between D and D♯.*

### Vintage mouthpieces

The older a horn is, the harder it will be to find it a matching mouthpiece. Modern mouthpieces usually don't work well with the vintage saxes. First of all, they don't make them sound like vintage saxes. Also, certain notes may not respond well, and the entire instrument can sound out of balance or out of tune. Vintage mouthpieces are usually shorter and may have extremely round chambers, rather than the modern, 'straight' type of chamber, as you can see below.

Modern

Vintage

*Vintage mouthpieces (below) often have a large, round chamber.*

### Many years

And finally: If you find yourself a good vintage horn and take good care of it, it will retain its value for many years — and it may even increase. On the other hand, musical instruments are usually not the best investments if you want to enlarge your capital.

# 7

# Mouthpieces and ligatures

Next to the reed, the mouthpiece is the most important part of your instrument. A well-chosen mouthpiece allows you to play everything you want to play as effortlessly as possible. The ligature plays a role too, both in the sound and the playability of your saxophone.

For beginners, the best mouthpiece is one that allows you to play as easily as possible. If you've been playing longer, you'll try to find a mouthpiece that allows you to effortlessly do everything you want to — playing loud and soft, low and high, short and long notes, with a fast response and the resistance and timbre you're looking for. Usually, that won't be the same mouthpiece as the one you started out on.

### A good fit

Just like a pair of shoes, a mouthpiece has to be a perfect fit. What fits you, when it comes to mouthpieces, is determined by your technique, your embouchure, and, eventually, the sound you're looking for.

*A mouthpiece shown from the side, from below, and in cross-section.*

Ligature

Tip opening

Facing length — Reed

Window

Rails

Facing

Bore

Cork

Baffle

Chamber

### How it works

The vibration of the reed causes the air inside the mouthpiece to vibrate. The resulting sound has a lot to do with the design of the mouthpiece.

84

An example? Your voice sounds different in a restroom than it does in the average living room. A mouthpiece has a 'room' too: the *chamber*. A different chamber will make for a different sound.

### The main parts

These are the main elements of a mouthpiece:
- The *tip opening* is the space between the tip of the reed and the tip of the mouthpiece.
- The *facing length* or *lay* is the distance from the tip opening to where the reed first touches the mouthpiece.
- The *window* is the opening under the reed. Look through the window, and you'll see the chamber.
- The neck enters the mouthpiece at the *bore* or *barrel*.

### Dimensions or words?

Mouthpiece specifications usually feature the exact sizes of the tip opening and facing length of each mouthpiece. On their own, these figures don't tell you too much, though: A mouthpiece has many more dimensions that affect its performance. So it's often more useful to read what mouthpiece makers say about the sound you can expect from a certain mouthpiece, and about the style of music for which it has been designed. An intimate, controlled sound for classical music. Or a sound that blends well, for ensemble playing. Or lots of volume and projection for wind bands that play outdoors, or great flexibility and expressiveness for jazz.

### Open or close

Sax players talk about *open* or *close* mouthpieces. An open mouthpiece, with a large tip opening, makes for a bigger sound. This requires a good embouchure and well-developed breath control. A close mouthpiece, with a small tip opening, plays more easily, and creates a less open, more controlled type of sound.

### Beginners

Most beginners start with a medium-close mouthpiece. Well-designed beginner's mouthpieces help you to play with

85

little effort and to learn to voice the notes accurately. Budget saxophones don't always come with a mouthpiece that qualifies as 'good,' however, and it often pays off to change it for one that does — even at a higher price.

TIP

### Reed-friendly

*A good beginner's mouthpiece is reed-friendly: Most reeds work well on them.*

### Big opening

Not every mouthpiece/reed combination that plays easily is a good choice for beginners. For example, you may find 'student' mouthpieces with a large tip opening and a soft reed, which play very easily. However, this combination makes it hard to voice the notes and to develop a good sound.

### Hundreds

Once you've been playing for a couple of years, you can enhance your sound with a professional mouthpiece — and there are literally hundreds to choose from. Depending on how well you play, what and how you play, and what you're looking for, you can easily make a basic selection of a handful of mouthpieces, or have a salesperson make a pre-selection for you.

### Comparing

Comparing mouthpieces is not very different from comparing saxophones (see pages 72–75). Always try mouthpieces on your own instrument, as they are very likely to behave differently on another horn. One extra tip: You may want to use a mouthpiece disinfectant to prevent rashes and other symptoms.

### The price tag

The price can also be a deciding factor in your choice. There are fine mouthpieces that sell for less than fifty dollars, but be prepared to pay up to a hundred or more. Professionals sometimes spend two hundred to more than a thousand dollars for special designs.

# THE DIFFERENCES

How a mouthpiece plays and sounds depends on the tip opening, the length and curvature of the facing, the size and shape of the chamber, and much else besides.

### Different ideas

Almost every mouthpiece company seems to have its own ideas when it comes to mouthpiece classifications, and to how 'open' and 'close' mouthpieces relate to one another. For example, with some brands the facing length increases proportionately with the tip opening.
Other makers offer two or three facing lengths, combined with a dozen different tip openings — and so on.

### Corresponding types

The way makers name their mouthpieces isn't very unambiguous either. An example? Most brands have an alto mouthpiece with a tip opening of 70/1000" (1.8 mm). Rico calls it a 3, Keilwerth calls it a 4, Dukoff a 5, Otto Link a 5*, and Selmer a C**... Only a few brands call this mouthpiece a "70" — and that's the number that directly refers to the actual size of the tip opening.

### Tables

Fortunately, to make your quest a bit easier, there are tables listing the characteristics of similar mouthpieces side by side. You can find them in music stores and on the Internet: Search for "mouthpiece comparison chart", and perhaps specify "saxophone".

TIP

### A higher number

One of the few consistencies in classifying mouthpieces is that a higher number or letter generally indicates a more open mouthpiece, within one make or series — so a 6 of one brand may still be more open than an 8 of another company.

87

### Asterisk

An asterisk is often used to indicate in-between sizes: A 5* ('five star') is between a 5 and a 6. Usually an asterisk refers to a larger tip opening, which is sometimes combined with a larger facing.

### Same opening, different sound

With mouthpieces, you can't simply line up the variables alongside one another and compare. After all, two mouthpieces with identical tip openings may be radically different, due to their respective chambers, facings, baffles, and so on. With that in mind, consider the following tips as a general guide.

# TIP OPENING

Differences between tip openings are quite large: For one type of sax, the largest opening is more than twice (!) as big as the smallest.

Tip openings for alto and tenor mouthpieces.

|  | Most commonly used | Very small | Very large |
|---|---|---|---|
| **Alto** | 70–100 (1.8–2.5mm) | 50 (1.3mm) | 125 (3.2mm) |
| **Tenor** | 90–120 (2–3mm) | 55 (1.4mm) | 145 (3.7mm) |

### A mouthpiece with a smaller tip opening:
- Produces a focused, 'smaller,' tighter sound;
- Is easier to control;
- Makes the instrument respond faster and speak easier;
- Is more suitable for classical music and for concert bands;
- Produces less volume and is easier to play softly;
- Requires a harder reed.

### A mouthpiece with a larger tip opening:
- Produces a larger, more open and muscular sound, with more body;
- Is harder to control (pitch, for one thing) and requires a better player;

- Is more suitable for jazz, rock, Latin, and similar styles;
- Produces more volume and is harder to play softly;
- Offers more possibilities for controlling the sound and the intonation;
- Requires a softer reed.

### A beginner?

For beginners, a mouthpiece with a relatively small to medium tip opening and a medium reed is often the best choice. The combination of a small tip opening and a hard reed isn't easy to play for a beginner. Combining a large tip opening with a soft reed will easily result in an unsteady sound.

### The hardest combination

A large tip opening with a hard reed is one of the hardest combinations to play on. It also produces the biggest sound, which is why you mainly find it on the horns of pro musicians in jazz, rock, and similar styles.

TIP

### Inches and millimeters

Tip openings are usually stated in thousandths of an inch, so 70 equals 70/1000" or .0070. If you want to convert this to millimeters, multiply by 0.0254 (0.0254 x 70 = 1.8 mm).

# THE FACING

A larger tip opening means the reed has to travel over a larger distance, which means that a larger part of the reed has to be able to vibrate. A longer facing or *lay* allows it that freedom.

### Curvature and facing

At least as important as its length is the facing's exact curvature. This specific dimension is usually not specified, the main reason being that it's hard to describe how 'curved' a facing is.

89

### A length for each opening

Mouthpieces are usually classified by their tip opening, and most manufacturers have a certain facing length for each tip opening they offer. In other words: The facing length often comes with the tip opening.

### A longer facing

Other makers offer mouthpieces with a choice of facing lengths for each tip opening. Many saxophonists feel that a longer facing adds more bottom or core to the sound, and that it makes a large tip opening easier to control. If it gets too long, however, it can render the sound dull and lifeless. In other words: A longer facing isn't always the solution for a weak tone.

TIP

## The measurements

*The facings of alto mouthpieces vary between approximately .600" (15 mm; very short) and .1000" (25 mm; very long). On tenor mouthpieces they roughly range between .670" (17 mm) and 1.175" (30 mm). Facing lengths are usually stated in tenths of an inch. To get millimeters, multiply by 25.4.*

### The rails

The edges or *rails* of the mouthpiece are also part of the facing. If the *side rails* are not exactly the same shape and thickness, the mouthpiece will be out of balance. As a result, you may get squeaks, or your instrument may have a poor response or a shrill sound.

Window

Tip rail

Side rails

### Thick rails, fat sound

The thickness of the side rails and the tip rail also affect the tone. If you're an advanced player, narrow rails will help you produce a bright, clear, crisp sound. For less experienced musicians such rails increase the risk of squeaks and an edgy, shrill tone. Thicker rails will get you a less brilliant, darker, fatter sound, and they make playing softly a little easier. Cheap mouthpieces generally have thicker rails — not so much for their tonal or playing characteristics, but because they are easier to produce.

### Smooth

The rails should always be perfectly smooth. The *tip rail* should have the same shape as the tip of the reed, and the side rails should have the same thickness and curvature left and right. This is often one of the problem areas for cheap plastic mouthpieces.

# CHAMBERS AND BAFFLES

Many brands offer a choice of chamber sizes — another important variable. At least as important is whether the mouthpiece has a baffle.

### Chambers

A larger chamber generally gives a darker, warmer, rounder, mellower sound, which blends well. It also makes for a more versatile mouthpiece that allows you more control over your timbre. With a smaller chamber you basically get a 'smaller,' more focused, tighter, edgier type of sound with the ability to cut through the music. High notes speak easier; low notes a little harder.

### Just the chamber

Some companies offer series of mouthpieces that differ in chamber size only, in order to allow you to change your sound without having to adapt your embouchure to another tip opening or facing.

**91**

### The baffle

The effect of a *baffle* can be compared to what happens if you squeeze the end of a garden hose, producing a more forceful, focused water jet: A mouthpiece with a baffle makes your sound more forceful and focused, with a brighter and edgier timbre. The higher the baffle, the more it will funnel your air stream and the stronger its effect will be. A mouthpiece with very little or no baffle helps to produce a smoother and warmer, more controllable and ensemble-oriented sound.

### Who's using what

Of course, there's a relationship between baffle and chamber size: The larger the baffle, the smaller the chamber becomes. As you may have figured out from the above, classical players usually use mouthpieces with larger chambers and no baffles, while saxophonists who need a bright, penetrating sound will usually go for small chambers and large baffles.

*Various baffles (Vandoren).*

### Self-adhesive or adjustable

If you want to experiment with the effect of a baffle, get yourself a set of self-adhesive baffles. They won't do the same as a baffle that was carefully designed within the context of the mouthpiece, but you'll get the idea. Also, there are mouthpieces with an adjustable baffle, which allows you to alter your sound to meet different room acoustics or musical situations — a brighter sound for a 'deader' sounding room or solo work, for example, or a smoother tone for ensemble playing.

### Throat

If you look through the barrel of a mouthpiece, at the opposite end from the tip, you'll see the shape of the *throat*. The larger the

92

throat, the darker, smoother, and warmer the sound will be. A smaller throat makes for a brighter, edgier type of sound.

### Free blowing
The throat also helps determine the playing resistance of the mouthpiece. Some saxophonists prefer a very free-blowing mouthpiece, while others like to feel some resistance — a choice that may have to do with your lung capacity as well.

### Round or square
Throats may be round, square, or square with rounded corners. The influence of this shape can't be considered separately from the other dimensions of the mouthpiece — which helps explain why some experts consider a round model ideal for unrestricted, free air flow, while others make the same claim for square ones…

# MATERIALS

Most mouthpieces are made of either hard rubber or metal. Hard rubber, also known as *ebonite*, is the most common material for classical and all-round mouthpieces. Metal mouthpieces are more often used by advanced jazz and rock musicians. However, there are also edgy-sounding hard rubber mouthpieces, just as there are metal mouthpieces for classical saxophonists.

### Size over matter
This shows that the material is not the most critical factor in affecting the instrument's sound. Though most mouthpiece makers choose metal for their 'bright and powerful' designs, the dimensions of the mouthpiece play a greater role in producing that timbre. It follows that you can't simply say that bronze mouthpieces sound darker than steel ones, for instance.

### Size difference
Playing a metal mouthpiece feels very different from playing a rubber one. Not only because metal just 'feels' different, but

93

also because metal mouthpieces have smaller outer dimensions than hard rubber ones. Some players like this, others don't. Soundwise, the fact that your mouth is less open when using a metal mouthpiece may contribute to the slightly more focused, tighter sound these mouthpieces are known for.

**TIP**

> ## Noisy
>
> *Playing a metal mouthpiece may produce unwanted noise due to moisture that collects inside: Your breath easily condenses on this material, especially — but not only — when it's cold. This is one more reason that you hardly ever see metal mouthpieces used by classical musicians.*

### Plastic
Good plastic mouthpieces can be made, but this material is typically used for the cheapest models, as it allows for easy and fast production. Low-budget saxophones often come with plastic mouthpieces. Note that there are professional synthetic mouthpieces as well, made of polycarbonate, for example.

### Other materials
Some manufacturers use other materials, such as a mix of graphite and synthetics, and a few even make wood, crystal, or ceramic mouthpieces. Some companies sell mouthpieces in various colors.

### Bite plate
The vibration of a metal mouthpiece is rather strong. To reduce the effect that these vibrations have on your upper teeth, most metal mouthpieces have a hard rubber *bite plate*.

### Mouthpiece cushions
Is the vibration still too much? Then use one or two *mouthpiece cushions*. These soft, self-adhesive patches are used on other types of mouthpieces as well, for example to prevent teeth marks on ebonite or plastic models. Mouthpiece cushions also enhance a stable embouchure by helping you keep your mouthpiece

from sliding to different positions in your mouth. They come separately or in sets, and in different hardnesses and thicknesses. Some brands adhere better than others. Finding the cushions that work best for you is a matter of trial and error, but they're not expensive.

### A *different sound?*
Many saxophonists feel that using mouthpiece cushions alters your sound. This is mainly because you perceive your sound differently, as the cushion muffles the vibrations that pass on through your teeth and skull. Someone else, in other words, won't hear the difference.

## MOUTHPIECE BUYING TIPS

- If your sax doesn't play well, **have it checked** before trying to solve the problem by buying a new mouthpiece. Also make sure the problem is not your choice of reeds — or your playing.

- Always keep your embouchure and level of development in mind when buying a mouthpiece, and try to avoid buying **one you can't handle** because of a tip opening, facing, baffle, or chamber that's either too large or too small.

- If you **play other woodwinds** as well, this may influence your choice: If the best saxophone mouthpiece you can find bothers you when changing to and from the clarinet, for example, you may have to decide to buy another one.

- Choosing the perfect mouthpiece quickly will always be difficult: You only really get to know a new mouthpiece after **a few weeks' playing**.

- A tuning line on the neck cork (see page 122) won't be of much use when play-testing mouthpieces, as they can differ in length. **Tune your sax for every new mouthpiece**.

- **Used mouthpieces** are available too. Always clean them before you try them, and carefully inspect them for dents,

95

chips, and other damage — especially the rails.

• When it comes to mouthpieces, **thousandths of an inch** can make a difference. That's why no two mouthpieces are exactly the same — even if they are 'identical' — so always try out a few before you decide.

### Mouthpieces and reeds

• When you are testing mouthpieces, be sure to always use **a good, new reed**.

• A new mouthpiece may require **different reeds** than the ones you were using — harder reeds, softer ones, or even reeds of a different brand.

• Note that some mouthpieces are more **reed-friendly** than others. With one mouthpiece, eight out of ten reeds will do well, while another makes you reject five out of ten.

• Also, a mouthpiece won't perform to its full potential until you have found the right reed to go with it. A good salesperson can advise you on good **reed/mouthpiece combinations**.

### Brand names

There are dozens of mouthpiece makers. Most saxophone makers have their own mouthpieces, which they don't always produce themselves. Many other, smaller companies specialize in mouthpieces, some of the better-known names being JJ Babbitt (Meyer, Guy Hawkins, Otto Link, Wolfe Tayne), Bari, Berg Larsen, Dukoff, Hite, Lakey, Lamberson, François Louis, Ponzol, Rousseau, and Runyon. Companies such as Brancher and Vandoren make both mouthpieces and reeds. Some of these companies offer mouthpieces for every style of music, and in various price ranges, while others are mostly known for their loud and bright-sounding mouthpieces, or for ensemble-oriented models, or for expensive or beginners' mouthpieces only. Still others feature special designs such as an adjustable lay, an integrated ligature, or a built-in metal reed that enhances the tone and loudness of your sax.

### How many?

Some saxophonists buy a good mouthpiece once and play it for the rest of their lives. Others never stop trying new models, brands, and types. Likewise, there are those who have a vast collection of mouthpieces to adapt their sound to different halls, groups, or styles of music, while others handle a similar variety of situations with just one mouthpiece…

# LIGATURES

Even the ligature contributes to your sound. Ligatures mainly differ in the material used, and in how they hold the reed — but there's more. Some ligature types and brands claim to improve the playability of your reeds, turning 'unplayable' reeds into playable ones, and to make reeds last longer.

### One or two

Some ligatures use two tightening screws for the reed; others have only one. The difference is not that big. One-screw designs are easier to attach or remove. Two screws are sometimes said to ensure a more even distribution of pressure across the reed — but one-screw designs can be just as good or even better.

### Inverted

An *inverted ligature* has its tightening screws not in the usual location, at the bottom of the mouthpiece, but on top, opposite the reed. This supposedly allows the reed to move more freely, and therefore to respond more easily.

### Material

Besides conventional metal ligatures, there are models in leather, soft plastic, fabric, metal mesh, and metal wire. The softer and thicker the material, the more it will tend to make your horn sound darker, warmer, and smoother. If you want to hear what a soft ligature can do for you, try attaching your reed with a shoestring or a piece of duct tape.

### Interchangeable plates

The smaller the contact area between ligature and reed, the more freely it can vibrate. This makes for a bright, open sound and a fast response. Some ligatures have interchangeable plates that hold the reed in various ways — with metal strips, or with four small points only, for example — allowing you to adapt your sound to the music or the venue.

*A standard metal ligature and a soft one (BG).*

### Tips and tricks

Standard ligatures can also be 'adjusted,' to some extent. If you have a reed that is a bit too light, tighten the upper screw a bit less. That allows a longer section of the reed to vibrate, which has an effect similar to that of a slightly heavier reed. There are more tips and tricks on mounting reeds in Chapter 9, Before and after.

### Bite

Two more things to pay attention to: Some types of ligature allow you to vary the exact position of the reed very easily, even without (re)moving the ligature itself. Others don't. Another difference is that some ligatures 'bite' into the reed. Once a reed has been fixed, it won't be easy to change its position again.

98

### A neat fit

Whichever ligature you choose, make sure it fits your mouthpiece. With a poorly fitting ligature the reed may slip out of place, or not seal to the mouthpiece correctly. A tip: A different ligature usually requires a different mouthpiece cap.

### Prices

The cheapest standard ligatures are available for five to ten dollars. Expect to pay ten to twenty if you want something better; professional ligatures are usually sixty dollars and up.

### Brands

Almost all saxophone and mouthpiece makers and some reed makers have their own ligatures, and there are also specialized accessory makers such as BG, Harrison, Oleg, Rovner, Runyon, Tru-Blo, and Winslow.

# 8

# Reeds

*What strings are to guitarists and violinists, reeds are to saxophonists. They are important for the way you sound and play, you need to replace them frequently, and there are all kinds of tricks to make them last as long as possible.*

The main difference between one reed and the other is how soft or hard they are. Most manufacturers classify their reeds with numbers, usually from 1 to 5, in half steps. The higher the number, the harder or more resistant the reed.

### Harder

Harder reeds allow for a louder, heavier, darker, thicker, or fuller sound, and they enhance the projection in the upper registers of the instrument without sacrificing tone texture. That said, harder reeds require good breath support and a developed embouchure, and they make it harder to play low pitches softly.

### Softer

Softer reeds make playing softly easier, and they promote a bright, transparent sound. If a reed is too soft, the sound may get very thin or buzzy. With soft reeds, chances are that your pitch will go up and down as you play, so it's harder to play in tune. Soft reeds speak easily — but if a reed speaks too easily, it may be hard to execute soft entrances in the upper register.

*Each reed consists of innumerable hollow tubes or fibers, as can be clearly seen at the butt.*

**TIP**

### Same thickness

*Contrary to common belief, a 2-strength reed is not thinner than a #4 reed of the same brand and series. It's simply made of a softer, less resistant piece of cane. Softer reeds have a shorter play life. Eventually, most saxophonists go for a 3, a 3H, or an even harder reed.*

102

## Number two?

Good to know: A reed #2 from one brand or series may be equivalent to a 1H or a 2H from another brand or series. As with mouthpieces, there are tables that list various types of reeds side by side. Some brands use names (*e.g.*, soft, medium, hard, etc.) instead of numbers.

## Your mouthpiece

Which reed to choose depends on various factors, your mouthpiece being one of them. For example, a smaller tip opening requires a heavier reed. With a reed that's too soft, it will close up and not respond at all. Conversely, a mouthpiece with a large tip opening will play easier with a lighter reed. For beginners the best choice often is a medium-soft reed, such as a 2 or a 2H, on a mouthpiece with a medium-small tip opening.

## Good and bad

Almost every box of reeds contains great reeds and good reeds, average and poor ones. If the boxes you buy seem consistently short of good reeds, try a different brand or a different type — and be sure that the problem doesn't lie somewhere else. If your mouthpiece is crooked or damaged, or if your instrument is leaking, any reed will seem poor.

## Not equally hard

Of course ten 'identical' reeds from one and the same box won't all be equally hard. A box of reeds #2H will contain reeds that are just a little harder than a 'hard' 2, as well as some that come close to a 'soft' 3.

## Thicker, steeper

How a reed plays and sounds also depends on its design: the thickness of the heart, the way it slopes toward the edges, and so on.

## French and American cuts

For example, reeds can be divided into *French cut* and *American cut* reeds. French cut reeds, which are mainly used by classical saxophonists, have a thinner tip and they're a bit thicker in the heart area. Reeds with an American cut usually feature a slightly thicker tip and less heart, which produces a more massive, focused sound.

### American?

However, these terms are not as neatly defined as they may seem. Just take a close look at a number of 'American cut' reeds from a variety of brands, and you'll find at least as many differences as similarities.

### French file cut

Reeds with a *file cut* or *double cut* have an extra strip of the bark removed, in a straight line, right behind the vamp. This enhances the flexibility of the reed, making for an easier response, especially in the low register. Also it helps produce a brighter, more narrowly focused sound. As this technique was developed in France, where classical musicians have always appreciated a brighter sound, it's known as *French file cut* — which shouldn't be mixed up with the French cut reeds mentioned above. The 'regular' or *unfiled* cut is sometimes referred to as *single cut*.

*Reeds without and with a (French) file cut.*

### Fine-tuning

The choice between filed and unfiled reeds can help you fine-tune your sound, regardless of the style you're playing. Saxophonists with a darker-sounding mouthpiece may want to use filed reeds, while unfiled reeds are often used on mouthpieces that tend to produce a brighter sound.

## Many more

Of course there are many more bigger and smaller differences. Some types of reeds have been developed for a well-rounded, centered, classical sound, while others are meant to blow easily with lots of color, expressiveness, and volume. Likewise, some reeds can handle fast phrases and powerful licks better than others that are better suited for performing long, steady notes — and so on. Most companies offer helpful descriptions of what their various designs were meant for. However, don't be surprised if you meet musicians who successfully use reeds that were designed for a completely different style of playing than theirs.

### What type of reed?

*Each brand makes different types of reeds. The only way to find out which reed you like best is to try a lot of them. And it can help to can trade experiences with other saxophonists too, but remember that no two players are alike. Also, a reed that works brilliantly with one mouthpiece can be hopeless on another. Another tip: Always try a couple of reeds of each type. One poor reed in a box of five or ten tells you nothing.*

## Prices

Most saxophonists who have found 'their' reed buy them in boxes of five or ten. Soprano, alto, and tenor reeds typically cost between two and four dollars each, and you may be able to get them for a bit less. Baritone reeds often start around four dollars.

# EXAMINING REEDS

You'll find good, average, and poor reeds in almost every box. Careful examination can often weed out the bad ones pretty easily.

### Inverted V

If you hold up a reed to the light, you'll see an inverted V. That V must be centered, and the reed should get thinner evenly to both sides. 'Crooked' reeds may squeak, and they're hard to play.

| Centered V-shape: good. | A 'crooked' reed: risk of squeaks. | Uneven grain: better to avoid such reeds. | Knots: reed vibrates unevenly. |

### Flexibility

By carefully sliding your thumb and index finger along the sides of the reed, you can tell whether the flexibility of the reed is the same on both sides.

### Too young

The color of a good reed varies between gold-yellow and gold-brown. If there's a hint of green, the reed may be too young. Young reeds usually won't last long or play well, if at all. Do not reject them right away, but let them sit for a few months at least.

### Grain and knots

The grain should be even throughout the reed, with the fibers densely packed, running evenly and parallel to one another. Reeds with spots and knots are unlikely to vibrate evenly.

### Wet it first

You won't know how good a reed is until you have been playing it for a while. A dry reed doesn't vibrate properly, so always wet it first. Keep it in your mouth for a while or put it in a glass of clean, lukewarm water for a few minutes. The latter method may extend the life of a reed: Some say water is better for reeds than saliva — but others disagree. Tip: Also available are reeds that are individually sealed in a humidity barrier packaging. Such reeds are ready to play instantly.

**TIP**

### Double plus, double minus

When you're testing a box of new reeds, give each reed a grade, or give the best reeds two plusses, the worst ones two minuses, and so on. Don't throw away the 'bad' reeds, but let them sit for a few months: Sometimes they will improve with age, and they never get too old. You can also try adjusting the poorer ones, or experiment a little with the placement of the reed on the mouthpiece (see page 117).

### Glass

You can also lay the reed on a wet piece of glass or mirror. Some reed cases have a special bottom for this purpose. The glass helps to keep the reed flat, removing waves or wrinkles at the tip. Don't use Plexiglas, as it's difficult to keep clean.

### Breaking them in

Reeds that perform very well straight away may not last very long. The best reeds are often the ones that seem a little hard to begin with. In other words, they don't play well right away. That's why some saxophonists first 'break in' their new reeds, for instance by only using them a few minutes per day for the first week. They may also use that breaking-in period to adjust the reed if necessary — a little bit every day. Some experts advise that you massage new reeds, sliding your thumb over the vamp, down to the tip, which may be helpful if a reed feels too stiff. Others don't bother with such procedures at all: If a reed doesn't play well, they simply take another one.

### Swapping reeds

Reeds are said to last longer if you don't use the same one for too long at a stretch. For that purpose, some sax players carry a supply of good reeds, which allows them to switch reeds every hour or even more frequently. Swapping reeds has yet another advantage: If you use one reed all the time, it will gradually become weaker. By the time the reed 'goes,' it will be so weak that any new reed you try will seem too hard.

### Suddenly

If you rotate your reeds regularly, you will also get a better feel for the slight differences between 'identical' reeds. What's more, you'll always have plenty of good reeds on hand — which is useful, because even the best reed can give up suddenly.

### Different reeds

You can also use these slight differences (or even use different strengths or types of reeds) to adapt to various playing conditions — for example, a harder-playing reed when humidity is very high, or in resonant or large venues. A lighter-playing reed works better in dry air, dry acoustics, and small rooms. In other words: The reed that sounds great in a small, insulated practice studio may not be the best reed for your next concert.

# ADJUSTING REEDS

Some saxophonists adjust every reed themselves; others do so only if it is really necessary, or not at all. Learning to adjust reeds takes a lot of time and patience, and you'll use up a lot of — bad or average — reeds doing it. A few important tips are listed below; some of the books on pages 178–179 discuss this subject at greater length.

### Higher, lower, or crooked

Before adjusting a reed, try to solve the problem by varying its exact position on the mouthpiece. A reed that doesn't seem to work well when it is put on perfectly straight may suddenly start sounding good if you mount it a little higher, a little lower, or at a slight angle — in which case adjustment will no longer be necessary. Want to know more? See page 117.

### Flat

If a reed's *facing* (the part in contact with the mouthpiece) is not perfectly flat or even, you can sand it down. Lay a piece of very fine grade sandpaper (number 320 or finer) on a small plate of glass to make sure it is level, or get a whetstone (*carborundum stone*) instead. Move the reed over it lengthways along the grain of the reed, with smooth and even motions, or carefully sand it in a circular motion, both clockwise and counterclockwise. Exert as little pressure as possible and don't let the tip touch the stone. Some people scour the reed with a sharp penknife instead, pulling the blade across the reed a few times.

TIPCODE

**Tipcode SAX-012**
*This* Tipcode demonstrates two ways to adjust a reed's facing.

### Too soft

A reed that's too soft can leave you with a messy, unsteady tone, or make a tone stop abruptly. The solution is to cut down the tip of the reed with a *reed cutter* or *reed trimmer*. Cut off as little as possible at first, and don't cut it down more than 0.04" to

**109**

0.06" (1–1.5 mm). Remember to first wet the reed. Afterwards, you may need to smooth the corners a little. To do so, use a file, always moving it towards the center of the reed. Most reed trimmers cost around twenty to fifty dollars.

TIPCODE

**Tipcode SAX-013**
*Here you can see how to use a reed trimmer.*

### Too hard

If a reed is too hard, you can make it more flexible by scraping it with a sharp knife or a piece of *reed rush* or *Dutch rush*, sold in music stores. Start in the areas marked with the figure 1 — carefully, because the reed is already very thin at this point. If necessary, go on to the areas marked 2, then to 3 and 4. Always remove equal amounts left and right, otherwise you will push the reed out of balance.

*Dutch rush or reed rush.*

TIPCODE

**Tipcode SAX-014**
*This Tipcode shows you how to use Dutch rush.*

## Shrill or dull

You can try rescuing a shrill-sounding reed by adjusting the areas marked 3 and 4. On dull-sounding reeds you start at 1, then move on to 3 and 4, and possibly try 2 as well.

### Squeak

*Squeaking reeds are often not equally flexible or thick on the left and the right. In the latter case you can try making the thicker edge a little thinner. Keep checking how much you have removed by blowing with the mouthpiece at an angle in your mouth: First try it left, then right.*

TIP

### Tips

• Work carefully: It's easy to remove **too much material**. For example, taking as little as a few ten thousandths of an inch off the tip of a reed makes it a whole 10% thinner!

• Frequently **check your results** as you work. Instead of constantly taking the ligature off and putting it back on again, you can temporarily hold the reed in place with your thumb.

• Some reeds will n**ever be any good**, however much you work on them.

• As a rule, avoid the area marked X, the **heart of the reed**.

• If you want to tackle the job really seriously, you can buy special **reed adjustment devices** and complete kits with prices up to three hundred dollars.

111

- And finally: **Waves at the tip** of the reed will typically disappear when you play it for a while, or if you briefly put the reed in a glass of water.

### Pith and saliva

A reed consists of countless hollow miniature tubes or fibers with a soft material (*pith*) between them. The pith becomes gradually softer from exposure to your saliva, until it gets so soft that the reed stops working altogether. How long that takes depends on the type of saliva you have, how often you play, and on the reed itself. Reeds typically last between two and six weeks.

### Increasing the lifetime

There are all kinds of ways you can try to increase the life expectancy of your reeds.

- Rinse your reed in **clean water** after playing. Then dry it, for instance with a cotton cloth or handkerchief, or by passing it between your thumb and index finger, always towards the tip. However, most saxophonists just dry the reed, without rinsing it first.

- Always store your reeds in a good **reed case** or **reed guard** (see pages 123–124).

- Lay each new reed on a flat surface and firmly rub it from the heart to the tip with the back of a teaspoon. This **closes the fibers** in the reed, which enhances its life expectancy.

- Don't play **the same** reed too long.

- **Break your reeds in**, so that the dried material gradually gets used to being wet again.

- A **hydrogen peroxide** solution (3%, available from your local drugstore) counteracts the effect of your saliva on the reed. Put your reeds in the solution overnight once in a while, and rinse them well before you use them again.

- **Never** set down a mouthpiece with a reed in it vertically. Lay it on its side, so that it can't fall over. That'll save on broken reeds.

- **Take a break**? A mouthpiece cap protects your reed and keeps it moist.

### Reed brands
Rico (US) also makes reeds under the LaVoz and Mitchell Lurie names. The companies Brancher, Glotin, Marca, Rigotti, Selmer (also makes saxes), and Vandoren (also makes mouthpieces) are from France, which is where most of the reed cane grows. Some other brand names are Alexander Superial, Daniel's, Olivieri, Peter Ponzol (makes mouthpieces too), Prestini, Reeds Australia, RKM, and Zonda.

### Synthetic reeds
Synthetic or plastic reeds are also available — for example, from the brands Bari, Fibracell, Hartmann (Fiberreed), and Légère. They last much longer than cane reeds, they're much more consistent, and they resist changes in temperature and humidity. This makes them great reeds for outdoor players. Another advantage is that you don't have to wet them before playing, which is especially easy if you have to switch instruments within one song. However, they are a good deal more expensive than cane, with prices from about seven or eight to twenty dollars each.

### Progress
The first synthetic reeds were often found to sound shrill, harsh, or edgy, and they were usually considered to be a less than ideal choice for beginning players: They could be quite resistant and hard to control, and they tended to cause intonation problems. In recent years, synthetic reeds have been so much improved that they are even being used by classical musicians.

### Taste
Both synthetic and coated reeds may be also considered if you don't like the taste of your cane reeds. Flavored reeds are also available, and there are bottles of reed flavoring that you can use to flavor your own reeds.

113

### Plastic coated reeds

As an alternative, there are plastic coated cane reeds. Basically, these reeds offer the same advantages as synthetic reeds do. Coated reeds tend to offer a quick response and a clear tone with great projection.

# 9

# *Before and after*

*A chapter about all the things you need to do to your saxophone before and after playing, from putting it together to tuning it, taking it apart, and storing it, with tips on amplification, stands, and lyres. Polishing, cleaning, adjusting, and other less frequent types of maintenance are dealt with in Chapter 10.*

To assemble your horn, start by attaching the reed to the mouthpiece, then put the mouthpiece on the neck and the neck on the body — but you can do it any other way around as well. This chapter starts with putting on the reed.

### In four steps

1. Slide the ligature onto the mouthpiece, holding it a bit higher than where it will eventually be positioned.
2. Slide the wetted reed (see page 107) under the ligature.
3. Make sure that the reed lines up with the mouthpiece, both at the tip and the sides. Then slide the ligature into position.
4. Tighten the ligature screw(s) — not too much, otherwise the reed won't vibrate properly.

*1. Slide the ligature over the mouthpiece until it's almost in its final position.*

*2. Place the wetted reed under the ligature...*

*3. ... and make sure the edges and the tip are exactly in line with the rails and tip of the mouthpiece*

*4. Now slide the ligature into place and tighten it — not too much, otherwise reed won't vibrate properly.*

116

**TIPCODE**

**Tipcode SAX-015**
This Tipcode shows you how to
put a reed on your mouthpiece.

### The ligature
Both the mouthpiece and the ligature are a bit wider on one end
than on the other, so always make sure you put the ligature on the
right way around. Many mouthpieces have a guideline that shows
you how far the ligature should be pushed down. Using another
type of ligature may render this line irrelevant, of course.

### Too light, too heavy?
You may vary the position of the ligature to compensate for a
reed that plays too lightly or too heavily. A reed will behave as
if it were a little harder if you slide down the ligature a bit, or
loosen the screw closest to the reed a little.

### Positioning the reed
You can also try moving the reed itself up (if it feels too soft) or
down the mouthpiece (if it feels too hard) a little. Reeds that are
not perfectly even left and right will often perform better if you
set them on your mouthpiece at a slight angle.

### Body and neck
The safest way to remove your sax from its case is to grasp it by
the bell with one hand, supporting it with the other. Don't grab
it by the key system, to prevent bending things. Put the neck into
the body with a gentle twisting motion. If the neck doesn't slide
into the body smoothly, clean the receiver (the top part of the
body) and the neck tenon with a dry cloth only. The small screw
of the receiver should, like the ligature screws, not be fastened
too tightly.

117

TIP

### Swivel

*Many saxophonists don't hold their horn directly in front of them, but off to the right a bit. To do so, swivel the neck slightly to the left. Make sure the octave mechanism is still lined up.*

### Cork grease

If the mouthpiece doesn't slide over the neck smoothly, the neck cork needs a little *cork grease*. Always have some with you (see pages 139–140).

### Warming up

A cold sax doesn't respond very well, and it will sound a little flat (too low). You can warm it up by blowing a few long, slow, silent breaths through the instrument, keeping all keys closed. If your sax has become very cold in transit, speed up the process by inserting a small towel into the bell.

### Brushing and flossing, food and drinks

If you want to spend as little time as possible on maintaining your instrument, then wash your hands and brush and floss your teeth before you play, don't eat during intermissions, and don't drink anything that contains sugar. It helps, really.

### The neckstrap

Adjust the neckstrap so that the mouthpiece swings directly to your mouth, without you having to stoop down or strain upward to reach it. If there's too much weight on your thumb, or if you have to face down, your neckstrap is too long — which may also hinder your sound. If you find yourself tilting your head backward, make the strap a bit longer. Invest some time to find the right neckstrap length: It may save you from chronic neck problems and other symptoms.

### Sticky pads?

Pads can stick, especially the ones that are closed when at rest. Short- and long-term remedies are covered on pages 138–139.

# TUNING

A saxophone needs to be tuned, even if you play by yourself. If you don't tune it, the instrument's intonation will be off.

### Adjusting the mouthpiece

You tune a sax by simply pushing the mouthpiece further onto the neck. This makes the entire instrument a bit shorter, and thus a bit higher in pitch. Moving the mouthpiece back makes the instrument longer, lowering the pitch. It's easy to remember: the longer the horn, the lower the pitch.

### Extreme tunings

If your horn is tuned way too high or too low, you may have intonation problems, as the position of the toneholes won't match the total length of the horn anymore. If the mouthpiece is too far back, your low register will sound sloppy as well.

### Concert A

Most orchestras and bands tune to the note A4. This is the A above Middle C on a piano.

### A=440

At this pitch the air vibrates 440 times per second, indicated as 440 hertz.

**TIPCODE**

**A4**

*Tipcode SAX-016*
*This Tipcode plays A=440 for about nine seconds. Not long enough? Press 'Play' again!*

### Tuning fork or metronome

Rather than using a piano, you can produce this reference pitch with a tuning fork. Tap it against your knee and set its stem on a tabletop, or hold it against or near your ear. Tuning forks are available in different tunings, so make sure you get one tuned to A=440. A tip: Most electronic metronomes and tuning devices can play this pitch too.

TIPCODE

**Tipcode SAX-017**
This Tipcode shows a tuning fork in action.

### Alto and tenor sax

•   To sound this A on an alto, you should finger an F♯, with the octave key depressed.

*An A on a keyboard.*

A

An A concert pitch on an alto (fingered F♯).

An A concert pitch on a tenor (fingered B).

- On a tenor you finger a B, also using the octave key.

### Tune to B♭

Some saxophonists prefer to tune to other pitches. One example is to tune an alto to a concert B♭, using a B♭ tuning fork. Why? Because you can finger the required G with one hand only, so you can play the tuning fork with the other. To tune a tenor or a soprano to this tuning fork, you have to finger a C.

### Far in, far out

If you're a beginner, it may be difficult to hear whether your instrument sounds flat or sharp. Here's a trick: First push the mouthpiece as far onto the neck as it will go. Now the instrument will sound obviously sharp. Then pull it out as far as possible, making it sound flat. The correct tuning will be somewhere in the middle.

**Tipcode SAX-018**
Pushing the mouthpiece onto the neck as far as it will go, will make the instrument sound obviously sharp, as this Tipcode clearly shows.

**TIPCODE**

### Electronic tuners

Most electronic tuners have a built-in microphone that 'hears' what you play and registers it on the dial as sharp, flat, or just right. Apart from tuning purposes, electronic tuners are also used to check an instrument's intonation or to practice voicing notes. Many experts disapprove of the latter, by the way: Electronic tuners (and keyboard instruments, for example) don't differentiate between an F♯ and a G♭.
Wind players should, though, for reasons that go beyond the scope of this book.

121

### Special tuners

*There are special tuners for transposing instruments. Shift it to the pitch your instrument is in and it will display the note you're fingering, rather than the sounding note. Another tip: Some tuners automatically switch off after a couple of minutes, which saves on batteries. Also, there are tuners that clip onto your instrument and respond to the vibrations of the horn instead of using a microphone. These allow you to tune in noisy surroundings.*

### Higher temperature, higher pitch

A sax will warm up with playing, so you may have to retune after a while: A higher temperature results in a higher pitch. If it's steaming hot or freezing cold, it may be hard to get the instrument to play in tune at all.

### Tuning line

Is your sax warmed up and well tuned? Draw a line on the neck cork or *tuning cork*, just where the mouthpiece ends. The next time you play, simply align the mouthpiece to the line. Then your tuning can't be that far off.

### Paper, thread, or match

If the tuning cork has gotten so compressed that your mouthpiece doesn't fit properly any more, simply wrap some thin paper around it. Cigarette paper is perfect. As an alternative you can wrap some thread around the cork, and then rub it with a candle. Others warm the cork with a lighter, for example. (Be careful, as cork burns easily.) The best solution is to have the neck recorked.

# AFTERWARDS

Taking proper care of your instrument when you're done playing will make it last longer — especially the pads — and it'll save spending time and money on more serious types of maintenance.

## Reed
Reeds last longest if you rinse and dry them after playing (see page 112). If you leave your reed on the mouthpiece, it won't dry as easily, which will make it more likely to warp. Besides, you'll have to take it off to wet it next time you play anyway.

## Reed cases
You can store your reeds in a very basic open reed holder or in a reed guard with some type of lid, both available for a couple of dollars. If you want something more luxurious, there are deluxe, leather-clad reed cases for fifty dollars or more.

### Numbered compartments
*If you tend to change your reeds frequently, or if you use different reeds for different situations, get a reed case with numbered compartments. This will help you to tell your reeds apart.*

## Wet, dry...
Reeds will dry most evenly in a reed case with ventilation holes and a ribbed floor, so that the air can get everywhere. Other cases have glass floors that help prevent your reeds from warping. What works best may depend on the reeds you use, and on how wet or dry they are when you store them.

## Humidity control
The best way to prevent warped and cracked reeds is to use some form of humidity control. Some holders have replaceable cartridges or inserts containing a substance that keeps the humidity at the right level. Alternatively, there are products such as the Reed Vitalizer, featuring a two-way humidity control that keeps your reeds flat by regulating the humidity automatically. As a result, reeds will play with more consistency too, and

123

they're always ready to play. Also available are special moisture-controlled cases, some even featuring built-in hygrometers.

*Various reed guards.*

Humidity regulator insert

### Low budget
A low-budget and less advanced alternative is to keep your reed guard in a freezer box or zip freezer bag, which will help to prevent the reeds from drying out. Tip: Reeds can go moldy if you keep them in a case that's completely closed.

### The inside of the instrument
When you play, the moisture in your breath condenses, wetting the inside of the instrument and the pads. To remove the moisture, you can use a swab, a pad saver, or both.

### Pad saver
A *pad saver* is a long fluffy plume that you move in and out of your sax a couple of times. Some saxophonists dislike pad savers because they tend to leave behind fibers that can stick on the pads or in the mechanism, because they may spread the moisture around rather than absorbing it, or because their rod can damage the inside of the body. Note, however, that pad savers come in different qualities. Prices start at about fifteen dollars. As an alternative, some use a wooden rod with a cloth attached to it.

124

Pad saver

## Pull-through swab

A pull-through swab consists of a cloth attached to a cord with a small weight on the other end. The cloth may be chamois, silk, or cotton. Simply drop the weight down the instrument and pull the swab through it a couple of times. The metal weight should be wrapped to prevent damage.

End plug

Swab

Weight

## Both

There are players who combine a swab and a pad saver, leaving the latter in the instrument once it has been dried with the first. Others, however, dislike the idea of leaving the pad saver in the horn, believing that it will collect dust and may dry out the pads too much.

## At home

Whether you use a pad saver or a swab, it's good to leave the case open just a bit once you come home. This allows the pads to dry slowly — unless air humidity is very low.

**125**

### The outside

To prevent stains and tarnish, it's advisable to wipe the instrument down with a soft, dry cloth after playing. Don't forget the neck and the little finger keys.

### End plug

The *end plug* protects the octave key rod — the small post that protrudes from the top of the body. End plugs can be made of rubber, plastic, metal, wood, or cork. Simply insert it into the body before packing up.

### The neck and mouthpiece

An ordinary handkerchief is all you need to dry the mouthpiece. It's even better if you rinse the mouthpiece in lukewarm water before you do. There are special swabs available too, both for the mouthpiece and the neck.

# CASES AND BAGS

Saxophone cases can be shaped (contoured or form-fitting cases) or rectangular, with a hard or a soft shell. Various materials are used to absorb shocks. A plush or velvet lining prevents scratching the instrument.

### More space

Good hard-shell cases usually have a strong plywood or molded plastic core. Rectangular models offer more space than shaped cases, with separate compartments for your neck, mouthpiece, strap, extra reeds, and accessories, and sometimes for sheet music as well. In a shaped case, usually featuring a hard plastic shell, the mouthpiece and neck often need to be stored in the bell (see page 128).

### Gig bag

A *gig bag* is a (heavily) padded bag, often made of water-resistant synthetic cloth, and subtly shaped for the instrument. Gig bags

A shaped
hard-shell case.

often have one or more extra pockets, as well as shoulder or
backpack straps. Most gig bags won't protect your instrument
as well as a good hard-shell case does, but gig bags are more
comfortable to carry around.

### Tight fit

To prevent damage, your horn should fit its case tightly, so that it
can't shift around. On the other hand, if the case is too small, it
can push too tightly against the instrument and bend its keys or
rods. For the same reason, never store sheet music on top of your
horn.

### Locked

Most cases can be locked. More than anything, these small locks
are there to prevent the lid from springing open if the case falls.
A separate case cover (*e.g.*, Cordura, canvas, leather) will do that
too, as well as offering additional protection against rain and
dirt.

**127**

### Locks and hinges
Check to see how sturdy latches, locks, zips, hinges, and handles are: They tend to be the weak points on cases and gig bags. Plastic clips and rings may not be as strong as metal ones.

### Neck and mouthpiece
If you store the neck and mouthpiece in the instrument's bell, you need to package them separately — and it's a good idea to do so if you store them elsewhere in your case too. There are special, inexpensive, high quality pouches with separate pockets for mouthpieces and necks, but many sax players simply wrap them up in lint-free cloths or gym socks.

**TIP**

### Preventing tarnish
To prevent silver-plated horns from tarnishing quickly, you can put special silver protectant paper strips in your case or bag.

### Prices
The cheapest gig bags are available for some fifty dollars or even less — but really cheap ones may be dangerous — moving up to three hundred or more for a genuine leather one. Decent alto or tenor cases, either rectangular or shaped, usually start around a hundred dollars, going up to three or four hundred dollars. Higher-priced cases are usually much more protective and can save lots of money in repairs.

### Key clamps
Very careful players may use *key clamps* or *sax clamps* when they pack their instrument: These sets of clips and pliers keep the open-standing keys closed for transportation, offering additional protection against bent keys and rods. They install and de-install in seconds.

### In or out
Storing your sax in its case or bag offers optimum protection and prevents airborne dust from clogging the key system. On the

**128**

other hand, if you leave your instrument unpacked at home, you can simply grab it, tune it if necessary, and play without having to put it together first. But please use a decent saxophone stand to prevent damage!

### Not too hot

Whether or not the instrument is in its case or bag, always make sure it doesn't get too hot, so keep it out of direct sunlight and away from other sources of heat.

# MISCELLANEOUS

A few odds and ends at the end of this chapter: neckstraps, saxophone stands, lyres, microphones, and some tips for on the road.

### Neckstraps

The traditional, narrow type of neckstrap isn't very comfortable. Many modern designs are considerably wider, and they often feature — sometimes removable — padding that evenly distributes the instrument's weight over your neck and shoulders. Other straps are designed to sit lower on your shoulders, rather than around your neck. Straps with a stretch backing are also available. Some musicians like the flexible feel; others don't.

### Harness and braces

If you want to avoid putting a strain on your neck entirely, buy a *harness*, which fits over your shoulders and around your waist. They may not be easy to get into or make you look great, but they're extremely comfortable and may save you a lot of pain. Harnesses or *dual shoulder straps* are particularly advisable for younger players. One more alternative are braces that attach to your clothes like a pair of suspenders. Prices range from less than ten dollars for a basic neckstrap to some fifty dollars for a harness.

**129**

A regular
neckstrap, a
brace, and a
harness.

## Hooks

Pay some attention to the hook too. Many saxophonists go for
the most straightforward type, basically a bent piece of hardened
steel wire with a plastic coating to keep it from scratching your
instrument.

A spring
hook, a snap
hook, and
a regular
hook.

## Spring hooks

Other hooks employ some kind of spring action. They're usually
considered to be more reliable, but they take more time when
changing instruments. Some of these hooks can swivel around
freely, so the strap doesn't get twisted.

### One hand

Watch out for the cheapest plastic hooks (they may break), and for hooks that may open inadvertently or allow the sax to work itself loose.

An important tip: Always support your sax with one hand when you're not playing, and don't rely entirely on the strap. Another one: Never carry your sax around holding it by the neck — it may come off.

### Saxophone support

There's an alternative for the neckstrap when you play sitting down: a saxophone support, consisting of a wide, curved Plexiglas strip that sits *under* your left upper leg and *over* your right upper leg. An adjustable hook mounted on the right-hand side of the strip supports the instrument.

*The Saxophone Support.*

### Mouthpiece cap

Intermission? Use a mouthpiece cap to protect your reed and keep it from drying out real quick. *Tip:* The Redi-Reed is a mouthpiece cap with a built-in sponge that keeps your reed ready to play. This is mainly helpful for doublers!

### Saxophone stand

Intermission? Always put your sax in a safe place — on a sax stand, for example. Good stands have soft bumpers and pretty long legs for stability; they are sturdy, easily collapsible, and easy to transport. Some can be raised to standing height, but this makes them a lot bigger, of course. Prices range from about twenty-five to fifty dollars. Double stands (*e.g.*, alto and tenor) and combination stands (*e.g.*, one or two saxes, and clarinet or flute) are available for doublers. Safety tip: On crowded stages it's advisable to attach the stand to the floor with duct tape.

*A saxophone stand.*

### Flip-folder and lyre

Marching sax players use a flip folder for their music, attached to the instrument by means of a so-called *lyre*. Many saxes have a lyre holder or lyre mount installed. If not, you can get a clamp-on lyre.

**132**

*A basic lyre.*

# MICROPHONES

If you play in an 'electric' band, your instrument needs to be amplified. For the occasional event you can use a good vocal microphone. If you need amplification more often, you may consider a dedicated saxophone miking system.

### Saxophone mics

Most of these systems use a small clip-on microphone that attaches to the rim or the back of the bell, often with a flexible gooseneck to adjust its position. Others have two microphones. Prices typically vary from around two to five hundred dollars. Wireless systems allow even more freedom to move around but they cost more.

### Preamplifier

Because the type of microphone used often produces a very weak signal, it usually needs a separate preamplifier — a small box that attaches to your clothing. The preamp, which usually features volume and tone controls, sends the signal to the power amplifier.

133

Sax microphone,
mounted on
the bell of the
instrument
(SD Systems).

### (Dis)advantages

These dedicated systems give you more freedom to move around than a microphone on a stand, without changing sound or volume. On the other hand, if your microphone is on a stand, you can deliberately influence volume and tone by changing the distance between the mic and your instrument.

**More?**

There's much more on microphones, wireless systems, and amplification in Tipbook Amplifiers and Effects!

## ON THE ROAD

Some additional safety tips:

• Don't put a saxophone on the **luggage shelf of a car**, under the rear window — especially not on a hot day.

• Getting out of the car? Always **take your instrument with you**.

134

- All kinds of things — including saxes — get **left behind** on the luggage racks of buses, trains, and subways. Tip: Keep hold of your instrument.

- Consider **insuring your instrument**, especially if you take it on the road — which includes visiting your teacher. Musical instruments fall under the insurance category of 'valuables.' A regular homeowner insurance policy will usually not cover all possible damage, whether it occurs at home, on the road, in the studio, or onstage.

- To get your instrument insured you'll need to know the **serial number** and some other details. You can list them on pages 212–213. Insurance companies also often ask for an appraisal report (see page 47) and proof of purchase.

# 10

# Cleaning and maintenance

*If you conscientiously follow the tips in the preceding chapter, your saxophone will require little further maintenance. A bit of extra cleaning now and again, and perhaps the odd drop of oil — that's all there is to it. Once in a while, though, you will need to take it to a technician for a COA (cleaning, oiling, and adjusting) or an overhaul. Here's what you can do yourself and what you should leave to a professional.*

To get rid of fingerprints and dust, wipe down the instrument with a dry or slightly damp, soft, lint-free cloth. Use a small soft brush for the tricky places, and be careful not to hurt your fingers: The needle springs are very sharp. This process is not cosmetic only: Dust may build up in the hinges and eventually clog up the key system, slowing down the action and causing excessive wear. To prevent dust from settling in the mechanism it's also advisable to vacuum your case once in a while.

### No polish

Don't use metal polishes on lacquered instruments. It wears down the lacquer coating in no time, and it can get into the hinges, gumming up the key system, and on the pads. On silver-plated saxes you may, very carefully, use a silver-polishing cloth once in a while: The extremely thin silver plating wears down easily.

### Your mouthpiece

Lukewarm water is often enough to clean your mouthpiece, and you may want to use a special mouthpiece brush, with some liquid hand soap or a mild dishwashing detergent. Adding a small amount of domestic cleaning vinegar works against the buildup of scale — and scale may very well hold disagreeable residues. Never leave a hard rubber mouthpiece in hot water or a vinegar solution. It won't fall apart, but chances are it will discolor.

### Swab and pad saver

A swab or pad saver gets a lot of junk out of your horn, so wash it from time to time with warm water and a mild detergent, and let it dry thoroughly.

### Sticking pads

Pads can stick — especially the ones that are closed when at rest. Fix them by sticking a piece of regular paper, a handkerchief, or a lens cleaning cloth under the pad, and then gently push the key cup down a few times. If that doesn't do the trick, try carefully pulling the paper out from under the pad while you keep it lightly closed with your finger on the key cup.

**Tipcode SAX-019**
This Tipcode shows you how to clean a pad with a piece of paper.

TIPCODE

*Stick it under the pad, close lightly, pull out...*

## Dollar bills, tissues, talcum powder
Instead of plain paper, a dollar bill may work even better, as it is a bit rough. Cigarette paper, good quality paper tissues, or a piece of paper coffee filter can be used too. Some saxophonists apply a bit of talcum powder to the pad with a Q-tip (cotton bud) or an old reed. However, the powder may render the pad even stickier when it gets moist. Also, it can find its way into the mechanism, where it can mix with the oil to form a sticky mass.

## Cork grease
Applying a bit of cork grease on the neck cork prevents it from

139

**TIP**

## Softening pads

Leather pads get harder with age. Various liquids, usually marketed as pad dope or pad juice, are available to help reduce this effect.

drying out, eases putting the mouthpiece on the neck, and provides a good seal. Cork grease comes in small containers and lipstick-type tubes. Some use Vaseline or light machine oils instead, but you can't go much cheaper than a two or three dollar tube of genuine cork grease, which has the added benefit of being designed for the purpose.

### Oiling the keywork

Music stores sell special cleaning sets for saxes. Besides a swab, a cloth, and one or two brushes, they often include a bottle of key oil. Some manufacturers advise you to put a *tiny* drop of oil on the hinges once a month or every two months.

### Don't do it yourself

Many technicians prefer you not to do that yourself, for one thing because oiling only really helps if you first take the mechanism apart and clean it. There's also the risk that you'll use too much oil or get oil on the pads, or use oil that is too thick or too runny for your instrument. So if you want to be on the safe side, leave it to an expert. Once a year or every six months is usually enough, if it's done properly.

### Doing it yourself

If you decide to do it yourself anyway, apply the oil with a pin: Drip a drop of oil onto a cigarette paper and dip your pin in it. That way you'll never use too much. As an alternative, there are special oil bottles with a hollow pin on the nozzle.

### On the road

There are a few tips that may help you when you're having troubles on the road, and there's no technician around.

- If a key suddenly **stops working**, look at the corresponding spring. If it's broken or gone, a rubber band may temporarily replace it. Always remove the rubber band after playing, as it may damage your plating or lacquer in the long run.

- Has the spring come loose? Then reinsert it. A **crochet needle** works well for this purpose.

- **Lost your low register?** Chances are that your neck octave vent does not properly close. Curing this often requires carefully bending the octave mechanism — which you may prefer to leave to your technician.

- Too much noise? Check for **missing bumpers**. You can reglue them with a drop of water-soluble glue. Other types of glue may harden your felts, spoil your finish, or be so permanent that felts and corks can't be replaced anymore.

- **Squeaks?** Wet the reed, replace the reed, or practice even more...

- **More useful things to take along** when you go out: a spare ligature and mouthpiece (rubber mouthpieces can break; metal ones can dent), cigarette paper, cork grease, a crochet needle, and a few rubber bands. For the technically inclined player there are special toolboxes available, filled with various spare parts and tools.

# CHECK-UP

If you get your instrument checked once a year, you can be fairly sure that nothing major can go wrong. Some technicians consider once every two years to be sufficient, depending on how much you play. Others recommend their customers to have the instrument checked at every drastic change of season. Expect to pay some fifty to seventy-five dollars for an annual checkup or COA (cleaning, oiling, adjusting). The longer you wait, the more expensive it can get. A tip: Many repair shops will give you a price and time estimate on the repair before checking your instrument into the shop.

141

TIP

### Sneaky leaks

*Most leaks develop gradually, and you don't notice them coming because you unconsciously adjust your technique to them, squeezing the keys a bit more, blowing a bit harder... Small leaks can often be cured by adjusting one or more keys, or by replacing one or more pads. A few tricks on how to locate leaks are on page 78.*

### Overhaul

Saxophones need to be overhauled once every five to ten years, mostly – again – depending on how much you play. A complete overhaul usually includes disassembling, cleaning, and degreasing the mechanism; cleaning the body and neck inside and out; removing small dents; leveling the toneholes if necessary; replacing pads, bumpers, and springs; and reassembling and adjusting the instrument. A professional job on a professional instrument may set you back some eight hundred to more than a thousand dollars. If you decide to have your instrument relacquered or replated, the overhaul is included, of course.

### A loan instrument

An overhaul usually means you'll be without your horn for at least a couple of days, and often even longer. Some music stores and repair facilities may provide you with a loan instrument while yours is in the shop. It pays to check this in advance.

### Try it out

Whether you take your instrument for a COA or a full overhaul, it will be adjusted. A tip: Try your instrument out before you take it home again, so that you know that it plays the way you want it to. Note that you may have to get used to the instrument feeling different, especially if the adjustment was way off.

# 11

# Back in time

The saxophone is one of the very few instruments that were actually invented, rather than developed over time, and it's only logical that it was named after its inventor. Adolphe Sax is best known for his saxophone, but he also invented and developed a host of other instruments and even some medical equipment.

Of the many stories about what Sax was really after when working on the saxophone, only one is correct: He wanted to create an instrument with the power of a brasswind instrument, the virtuoso possibilities and the flexibility of a string instrument, and the timbre and tonal flexibility of a woodwind instrument. One of his main inspirations was the *ophicleide*, a now obsolete brasswind instrument with a woodwind key system and a trumpet-like mouthpiece.

*Ophicleide.*

### The first one
Sax, born in Belgium in 1814, built his first 'Sax-o-phone' when he was in his mid-twenties. This horn had a range similar to that of the modern baritone sax. Originally, Sax referred to it as a bass saxophone. Around 1856 he gave his instruments their final names, as we know them today.

### Military bands
By that time, Sax had developed two saxophone families. The largest consisted of six B♭ and E♭ instruments, from the sopranino to the bass. These saxophones were designed to be used in military bands, where their timbre and potential for volume perfectly fit the format.

### Symphony orchestras
The other family consisted of four saxes: two in C (soprano and tenor), and two in F (alto and baritone). Their slightly

Adolphe Sax
(1814–1894).

more delicate sound — a result of the higher tuning — was created with the symphony orchestra in mind. However, once the instrument found its place in orchestral settings, most composers opted for B♭ and E♭ saxophones.

### Alone and a pauper

It was jazz musicians who made the sax really popular, when this style of music began to develop in the early 1900s. Too late for Adolphe Sax, unfortunately: He died in 1894, alone and a pauper, having fought many lawsuits against people who disputed his patents.

### Brass and bass clarinets

Besides the saxophone, Sax is also known for his work on various brass instruments (the saxhorns, *e.g.*, the tenor horn and the baritone), and on the bass clarinet.

**145**

# 12

# The family

*Even though saxophones are made of brass, they belong to the family of woodwind instruments, just like clarinets, oboes, and flutes. This chapter covers all the saxophone voices, some saxophone variations of the past, the main other woodwinds, and the electronic family members.*

The four most important saxophone voices have been mentioned and described in various chapters in this book. The three others are quite rare. The *sopranino* is even smaller than the soprano, and therefore higher in pitch.

sopranino (E♭)  Soprano (B♭)  Alto (E♭)

Tenor (B♭)  Baritone (E♭)  Bass (B♭)  Contra bass (E♭)

### Bass and contrabass
The *bass saxophone* sounds an octave lower than the tenor. The rare *contrabass* — the largest of them all — is an octave lower than the baritone.

### C melody
Over the years, many variations on these voices have been developed. One of the best-known examples is the *C melody*, basically a tenor in C. This instrument was extremely popular in the 1920s. Buying one now is usually not a good investment; too many were made to make them very valuable, and it's

A sopranino
and a bass
saxophone.

extremely hard to find matching reeds, mouthpieces, and other parts.

### One-handed horns

The same goes for a number of other saxophone variations, most of them built around that same era, such as the soprano sax in C, the sopranino in F, and the *saxello* — a straight B♭ soprano with a bell that pointed toward the audience. Another bell variation was featured on the Conn-O-Sax, a mezzo soprano in F with a bulb-shaped bell that had three additional resonance vents. Conn also made saxophones that could be played with one hand only. These instruments were mainly used in circuses and vaudeville acts.

### Plastic saxophone

The late Charlie Parker, one of the world's most famous jazz alto players, was known for using a wide variety of horns — and he always sounded like himself, even when he played the white Grafton saxophone, a horn with a plastic (!) body. The Grafton Acrylic Saxophone was available in the early 1950s.

TIPCODE

**Tipcode SAX-020**
Can you hear the difference? Play this Tipcode and hear a regular brass alto, and a plastic one by Grafton.

### Bamboo

Other saxophone varieties look even less like the original instrument. One example is the Bamboo Jim Brock Sax. The toneholes in the bamboo body of the instrument are closed with your fingers, just like a recorder, and it uses a regular saxophone mouthpiece.

# OTHER WOODWINDS

The only visible characteristic all woodwinds share is that they consist of a body with various toneholes. Opening and closing these toneholes produces various pitches. This explains why not only wooden instruments (clarinets, oboes, recorders, and so on) are woodwinds, but flutes and saxophones too. Woodwinds also share a certain tone quality or timbre, which is clearly different from that of brasswind instruments (trumpets, trombones, etc.).

### Reed instruments

Saxophones and some of the other woodwinds are also classified as *reed instruments*, for obvious reasons. Reed instruments come in two groups: Those with a single reed, such as the clarinet and the sax, and those with a double reed, such as the oboe and the bassoon.

### Clarinet

The clarinet is often considered the saxophone's closest relative, as they're both *single-reed instruments*: They have similar mouthpieces with a *single beating reed* — the reed 'beating' against the mouthpiece as it vibrates. The differences between clarinets and saxophones are quite large, though. First, the clarinet has a largely cylindrical body, which makes it sound and blow very differently. Second, the clarinet's register

**TIPCODE**

**Tipcode SAX-021**
This Tipcode demonstrates the timbre and sound of a clarinet.

151

key doesn't make notes sound an octave higher, but a twelfth. Third, its key system is quite different. Fourth, most clarinets have a wooden or synthetic body. Still, many musicians play both instruments.

*A clarinet has a largely cylindrical body.*

cylindrical narrower        cylindrical                    wider

### Oboe and bassoon

The oboe, like the sax, has a conical bore. On the other hand, the oboe resembles the clarinet, with its wooden body and its key system. At the same time, it's completely different from those two, because it's a *double-reed instrument*; it has two reeds that vibrate against each other, just like the bassoon, which sounds much lower, and the English horn. This makes it a completely different instrument. Not many musicians play both single- and double-reed instruments.

**Tipcode SAX-022**
*This Tipcode plays an oboe and a bassoon.*

### Flute

Flutes were originally made of wood, and many — mainly classical — flutists still prefer wooden instruments to the much more common metal ones. Piccolos, sounding an octave higher, are even more popular in wood, and also available with

152

A clarinet,
an oboe and
a flute.

**Tipcode SAX-023**
Play this Tipcode and you'll hear a concert flute.

plastic bodies. The flute's key system has similarities to that of a clarinet and a saxophone. The body is cylindrical, and there's no reed. Versatile woodwind players often play saxophone, clarinet, and flute.

# ELECTRONIC WIND INSTRUMENTS

Electronic wind instruments, introduced in the early 1970s, usually have a saxophone-style keywork and mouthpiece. You use them to control and play sounds from sound modules, synthesizers, or other electronic sound sources.

### Any sound, seven octaves
Using an electronic wind instrument, you can usually play any type of sound over a seven-octave range, you can play chords, and much more. Lip and wind pressure sensors can be used for different purposes (dynamics, effects, and so on).

### MIDI
This is usually done through MIDI, a standardized *musical instrument digital interface*. MIDI allows you to hook up synthesizers to computers, digital sound sources to effect devices and recording equipment, and so on.
Electronic wind instruments are often referred to as MIDI wind controllers.

154

## Examples

The original American Lyricon served as an example for many later designs. Well-known companies making MIDI wind instruments are Yamaha and Akai. The Synthophone, built inside an alto saxophone body, uses traditional saxophone fingerings.

*A Yamaha WX-5 MIDI controller and an Akai EWI 3020.*

# 13

# How they're made

*Traditionally, saxophones, mouthpieces, and reeds were made entirely by hand, of course — and some companies still do a lot of things that way. Here's a quick look at what's involved in the various production processes.*

The body and bell are produced from flat sheets of brass, which are folded double, soldered, and then formed using dies and presses. Some companies still have craftsmen doing this, however, using steel mandrels and wooden hammers. The neck is, simply put, a bent length of pipe.

*The traditional way: shaping the tube with a wooden hammer.*

### The toneholes

To make the toneholes, small holes are drilled into the body and the bell. Then a metal shaft is inserted into the tubing. This *spike* is inset with metal pulling balls, each one matched exactly to the size of the corresponding tonehole. These balls are pulled forcefully through the pre-drilled holes, forming the tonehole chimneys as they go. This technique is known as pulling, drawing, or extruding toneholes.

### Posts

Once the toneholes are ready, the posts are mounted on ribs and soldered onto the instrument.

### Finishing and assembly

The horn is cleaned and polished extensively before being lacquered or plated. The most common type of finish is an epoxy lacquer, which is baked on the horn. Assembling the horn includes installing the keywork and carefully seating the pads.

### Play-testing and adjusting

At the end of the process, the saxophone is play-tested and adjusted. The more expensive the instrument, the more attention

**TIPCODE**

**Tipcode SAX-024**
This Tipcode is a visit to a reed company, showing you how reeds are made from start to finish.

will usually be devoted to the final testing and adjusting stage. Most new saxes, however, need an extra shop-adjustment before they're really ready to play.

# REEDS AND MOUTHPIECES

Most reeds are made of Arundo donax, a type of cane that grows particularly well in southern France (the Var region), but also in South America, Australia, and elsewhere.

### Curing
The plants are harvested when they are two to three years old. By then they have usually grown to about 25 feet (eight meters). After harvesting, the cane is dried and cured for a year or more.

### By size and into shape
The tubes are chopped into short pieces and then sorted by size:

From cane to reed, showing four of the many steps.

159

larger ones for the big reeds used on baritones, smaller ones for tenors and altos, and so on. The tube lengths are split into four pieces, and each quarter is made into a reed using a series of machines and techniques — flattening and sanding, cutting the rough shape, removing the bark, profiling the reed, and cutting the tip. At each stage the reeds are inspected visually, and the bad ones discarded.

### Number
A special device measures the resistance of each reed at the tip. The higher the resistance, the harder the reed, and the higher the number it is given. Finally, the reeds are once again inspected thoroughly, stamped, and packed.

### Mouthpieces
The production process of a mouthpiece mainly consists of boring, reaming, smoothing, flattening, filing, sanding, buffing, polishing, and related treatments. In a series of steps the basic hard rubber or plastic mold is worked to exacting specifications, with tolerances of tens of thousandths of an inch — or even less. Metal mouthpieces, whether they start out as a solid block or as two forged pieces that are soldered together, undergo similar processes. In most companies a number of operations is undertaken by computer-controlled machines; others still require skilled handwork. The final steps include corking and stamping.

# 14

# Brands

*This chapter offers a brief introduction to the main saxophone brands you'll come across in music stores. At the end, some examples of well-known vintage horns are noted.*

There are more saxophone brands than saxophone makers: Various factories make instruments under more than one brand name (i.e., stencil instruments), and they supply horns for the private label instruments that are marketed by some of the larger dealers.

### The larger companies

This chapter starts with brief descriptions of the larger companies that make their own horns from start to finish, followed by a section on smaller and newer companies from various countries.

> ## Time sensitive
>
> *Note that the information in this chapter is more time-sensitive than the contents of any of the other chapters in this book: New brands are introduced from time to time, others are discontinued; factories are closed, brand names are sold — and so on.*

The first Buffet Crampon saxophones were made in 1866. The French company, independent again since 2005, produces student and professional saxophones, as well as clarinets, oboes and bassoons. Buffet Crampon also owns the brass wind companies Antoine Courtois Paris and Besson.

## ⊜ JUPITER.

Jupiter is one of the larger and older Asian saxophone makers. The company, which goes back to the 1930s, also produces a host of other woodwind and brasswind instruments.

Julius Keilwerth, founded in 1925, produces instruments in the middle-to-high price range. Keilwerth has always made instruments for other companies as well, both from Europe and the US.

The first Selmer saxophones were made in 1922. Six years later the French company bought the brand name Adolphe Sax Fils (Adolphe Sax's Son, literally). Besides pro saxes, the company also makes various brass instruments. Selmer established its name in America before World War II, at which time the firm cooperated with Buescher.

# Selmer®

The American Selmer company evolved from the French collaboration with Buescher. Though sharing the same name, the American and French companies are now independent. Selmer USA focuses on student and intermediate saxes, (formerly) marketed as Selmer Bundy and Selmer Signet, besides making other wind instruments.

Yamaha, which started as a one-man organ factory in 1889, is one of the few sax makers that offer horns in all price categories. The first Yamaha saxes were released in 1967. Yamaha also

163

makes all kinds of other instruments, as well as motorbikes, hi-fi equipment, and much more.

---

# YANAGISAWA ◀

Yanagisawa began making saxophones in 1954. At present the Japanese company only makes instruments in the higher price range. It's particularly well known for its sopranos, but makes all other voices and special necks as well.

### Medusa

The German company **B&S**, makers of **Medusa**, **Allora**, **Chicago Jazz**, and other brands, stopped making saxophones in the early 2000s.

### New US-made saxes

Today, only few companies are producing saxes in the US: The main names are **King**, **Conn**, and **Vito**, all focusing on the lower price ranges. **Oleg** focuses on the professional market, making instruments to custom order only.

### More American brands

Other American companies have their instruments partly or entirely made elsewhere — typically in Asian countries. Some of these companies take care of several parts of the production process in house, varying from assembly to adjusting and play-testing the horns. Companies such as **Barclay**, **Belmonte**, **Blessing**, **Giardinelli**, **Gulf**, **Kohlert**, **F.E. Olds**, **Palatino**, and **E.M. Winston** tend to focus on the lower price ranges. Other companies (also) market intermediate and/or professional instruments, such as **Antigua Winds**, **Cannonball**, **LA Sax**, **Prestini**, **Stephanhöuser**, and **Vespro**.

### Asia

Japan was the first Asian country that started mass production of high quality, affordable instruments. Taiwan followed pretty quickly. Two large Taiwanese companies that make saxophones as well as a host of other instruments are **Dixon** and, as mentioned above, **Jupiter**. **P. Mauriat** is a Taiwanese company that specializes in intermediate and professional saxophones.

### Other countries

Selmer Paris and Keilwerth are the best-known European saxophone makers, but they're not the only ones. Some of the others are the Czech **Amati** company; **Trevor James** from England; and the Italian makers **Borgani** (since 1872; one of the few companies that still makes hand-hammered horns), and **Rampone & Cazzani**. You may also come across Italian **Grassi** and **Orsi** saxophones. Many saxophone makers around the world use Italian made pads (e.g., **Pisoni**, **Prestini**. The latter makes saxophones too). **Weril** is a Brazilian company that also makes brass instruments and banjos.

# VINTAGE SAXES

Vintage saxes, built around or before the 1960s, can be quite valuable — but others aren't a good investment at all. Some series, for example, have known good and bad years; bad horns have been made in good years too; and not every horn has stood the test of time (or the sometimes indelicate techniques of the people who owned it) equally well. Please refer to specialized literature and contact saxophone stores for additional information, and for listings of serial numbers that show you exactly when a sax was built. These listings can also be found on the Internet (see page 180–181).

### Old American horns

Pretty much every 'old' American sax maker produced one or more horns that are still in demand. Some of these names may be found on new instruments too.

- **Conn**, the first American company to make saxophones (around 1888), became well known for saxophones such as the Naked Lady, the Ladyface, the Connquerer, the 10-M, and the (New Wonder) Chu Berry.

- **King**'s claims to fame were the Zephyr and the richly engraved Super 20, among others.

- **Ferdinand August Buescher**, who first worked for Conn, later produced his own instruments. The 400 and the 1940s Aristocrat are famous models.

- **Martin** was well-known for its soldered (rather than drawn) toneholes. The Committee, the Magna, and the Martin are some of the best known models of this brand. Martin also made a sax with mother-of-pearl keys all over, known as the Typewriter.

### Selmer

Examples of well-known vintage Selmers are the Cigar Cutter, the Super Action, and the Balanced Action. Their key mechanisms, compared to American-made saxes from that period, were quite advanced. The most famous sax of all time is probably the Selmer Mark VI, which was made from 1954 until the early 1970s. A good Mark VI, especially when made in the early 1960s or before, easily costs as much as or more than a new professional horn.

### Old for less

Other older saxes include popular student or intermediate instruments that offer decent quality for much less money. Some examples from the late 1950s until the late 1970s are the Martin Handcraft, the King Cleveland, the Selmer Bundy, the Conn PanAm, and the Conn USA. Instruments from that era by Armstrong and Vito may serve you well too, as will the King 613 and the Conn 16M.

### More names

Other names from the past include:

- **Couf** saxophones were made by Keilwerth for Herbert Couf, president of the Armstrong company, from 1965 to 1986.

- **Armstrong** currently makes flutes and piccolos only.

- **Holton**: Frank Holton was one of the first American saxophone makers. The company now makes brass instruments only.

- **Dolnet**, a French company that built saxes from the 1880s to the 1980s.

## *VINTAGE MOUTHPIECES*

Also, there's a market for older mouthpieces, some of which are highly prized by saxophonists who want that traditional, vintage sound — and they may cost as much or more than a new one. A few examples are old Berg Larsens, Otto Link mouthpieces from the 1950s, Dukoffs from the 1940s, and Brilharts from that same era. A tip: Just as new mouthpieces don't always work well with vintage saxophones, old mouthpieces may not fit new horns either (see pages 80–81).

# Glossary

This glossary contains brief definitions and descriptions of
the majority of saxophone related terms. Most terms are
explained in more details as they are introduced in this book.
Please consult the index on pages 214-216.

**Action**
The mechanical 'feel' of your sax.

**Altissimo**
Higher notes than the keys of your sax may seem to allow you. Also known as top tones or high harmonics.

**American cut reed**
A reed with a slightly thicker tip and less heart, as opposed to a French cut reed. See also: *French cut* and *French file cut.*

**Articulated G♯, Automatic G♯**
Opens the G♯ vent when low C♯, B, or B♭ are used.

**Baffle**
A 'bump' on the inside of the mouthpiece, making for a more aggressive, piercing sound. Also called wedge.

**Bari**
Short for baritone saxophone.

**Bell**
The flared opening of a saxophone.

**Bell keys**
The keys that open or close the large toneholes in the bell.

**Body**
If you remove the neck, the bow, the bell, and the key system, you are left with the saxophone's body, *i.e.*, the main 'tube' of the instrument.

**Booster**
Resonator: the metal or plastic disc

on the inside of a pad.

**Bore**
*1.* The internal dimensions of the mouthpiece, neck, body, bow, and bell.
*2.* The end of a mouthpiece, into which the neck fits.
*3.* Another word for the chamber of the mouthpiece.

**Bow**
The U-end between body and bell.

**Brace**
1. Reinforcement, connecting the body to the bell.
2. A suspender-like neckstrap.

**Cap**
Mouthpiece and reed protector.

**Chamber**
The internal space of a mouthpiece. Also referred to as bore.

**Conical bore**
A sax has a conical bore: It gets wider toward the bell.

**Crook**
British word for neck, the tube that connects mouthpiece and body.

**Doubler**
Someone who plays more than one (wind) instrument, *i.e.*, sax and clarinet, or sax and flute, or all three.

**Dutch rush**
A plant that grows in swamps, used for adjusting reeds. Also known as *reed rush.*

**Ebonite**
Most mouthpieces are made of ebonite, *i.e.*, hard (vulcanized) rubber.

**Embouchure**
The way you use your lips, jaws, tongue, and all the muscles around them when playing a wind instrument.

**Facing**
1. The area where the mouthpiece curves away from the reed. Also called lay.
2. The underside of a reed.

**French cut reeds**
Reeds with a relatively thin tip and a thicker heart area. See also: *American cut reed*.

**French file cut**
Special way of cutting reeds, making for a more open, brighter sound. Not to be confused with French cut.

**Front F**
A key to easily reach a high E, F, or F♯. Also referred to as quick F or forked F.

**Gooseneck**
See: *Neck, neckpipe*.

**Hard rubber**
Most mouthpieces are made of hard (vulcanized) rubber, also known as ebonite.

**High F♯**
Special key to play high F♯.

**High pitch**
Some older saxes have a higher tuning (*e.g.*, A=451 rather than A=440).

**Hook**
1 The hook on the neckstrap.
2. The supporting hook for your right thumb.

**HP**
See: *High pitch*.

**Intonation**
A sax with bad intonation will be difficult, if not impossible, to play in tune. A player who has bad intonation will play out of tune even on the best saxophone.

**Key cups**
The cups holding the pads that cover the toneholes.

**Key height**
The (adjustable) distance the keys open.

**Key risers**
Affordable way to raise keys that are too low for your fingers.

**Key system**
The saxophone's mechanism.

**Keys**
Keys allow you to open and close the saxophone's toneholes.

**Lay**
The area where the mouthpiece curves away from the reed. Also known as *facing*.

**Ligature** Holds the reed in place.

**Little finger keys**
The pinkie keys or touch plates that are operated with your left and right little fingers. Also referred to as plateau keys or table keys. The two groups of keys are known as plateaus, tables, or the low (right hand) and high (left hand) stacks.

**Microphones**
Vocal microphones work great for sax players. There are also dedicated sax mics that attach to the bell of the instrument.

**Mouthpiece**
The most crucial part of the instrument, together with the reed.

**Mouthpiece cushion, pad, patch**
Reduces the vibration of a (metal) mouthpiece against your teeth. Also used to protect mouthpieces against bite marks.

**Mute**
Designed to reduce the volume level of the instrument.

**Neck, neck pipe**
The tube that connects mouthpiece and body. Also referred to as gooseneck or (British) crook.

**Neck cork**
Cork sleeve at the end of the neck. Also referred to as tuning cork.

**Neckstrap**
Comes in a wide variety, from basic ones to harnesses.

**Octave key, octave vents**
The octave key 'automatically' opens the lower or the upper octave vent, depending on the note that you finger. Also known as register key: When you use this key, you move to a higher register.

**Pads**
Pads seal the toneholes.

**Pad saver**
A long, plush-covered rod, used to reduce the moisture in your instrument after playing.

**Palm keys**
Set of keys operated with the palm or the fingers of your left hand.

**Pearl keys**
Keys with pearl inlays.

**Pinkie keys**
The little finger keys or touch plates that are operated with your left and right little fingers. The pinkie keys are also referred to as plateau keys or table keys. Collectively, the two groups of keys are known as plateaus or tables.

**Plateau, plateau keys**
See: *Pinkie keys*

**Post construction**
See: *Rib construction.*

**Post mounting**
See: *Rib construction.*

**Posts**
Hold the key mechanism in place.

**Quick F**
A key to easily reach a high E, F, or F♯. Also referred to as front F or forked F.

**Rails**
The three edges (tip and side rails) of the mouthpiece window.

**Range**
The distance from the lowest to the highest notes on the instrument.

**Reed**
A carefully shaped piece of cane part that vibrates as you play, setting the air in motion and thus producing the basic sound of the instrument. A good reed should match both your way of playing and your mouthpiece.

**Reed instrument**
Saxophones belong to the group of reed instruments (or simply 'reeds'). They're also wind instruments. See: *Wind instrument*.

**Reed player**
Saxophonists are sometimes referred to as reed players — just like clarinetists, for example.

**Reed cutter**
Reed trimmer: reed adjustment tool.

**Reed guard**
Protective holder for reeds.

**Reed rush**
A plant that grows in swamps, used for adjusting reeds. Also known as *Dutch rush*.

**Reed trimmer**
Reed cutter: reed adjustment tool.

**Register**
The range of the saxophone is often broken down into three registers: low (all notes without octave key), middle (with octave key), and high (with octave key plus side keys).

**Register key**
See: *Octave key*.

**Resonator**
Metal or plastic disc on the inside of a pad. Sometimes referred to as booster.

**Rib construction, ribbed construction**
Saxes with a rib construction or ribbed construction have the posts attached to metal strips, rather than directly to the body (*i.e.*, post construction, post mounting).

**Sax, Adolphe**
The instrument's inventor (1814–1894).

**Side keys**
Set of keys on the lower right-hand side of the instrument, used to play high notes and trills.

**Side rails**
The side edges of the mouthpiece window.

**Spatula keys, spatulas**
Spatula-shaped keys. Used to refer to little finger keys and other keys.

173

**Springs**
Needle springs make the keys return to their original positions after you've played them.

**Stack**
To some, the low stack refers to the bottom (right hand) half of the key mechanism, and the high stack to the other half. To others, low and high stack refer to the right- and left-hand little finger keys, respectively. See: Little finger keys.

**Table**
1. The flat underside of the reed. 2. The flat part of the mouthpiece on which the reed lies. 3. The two groups of little finger keys, pinkie keys or table keys.

**Thumb hook**
The (possibly adjustable) hook for your right thumb, which helps support the saxophone.

**Thumb rest**
Your left thumb rests on the thumb rest, just below the octave key or register key.

**Thumb saver**
A soft sleeve to cover the thumb hook.

**Tilting keys**
Little finger keys that tilt toward the key that's being played. Special feature.

**Tip opening**
The distance between the tip of the reed and the tip of the mouthpiece.

**Toneholes**
The holes in the sax, also known as sound holes or vents.

**Touch plates**
The little finger keys or pinkie keys that are operated with your left and right little fingers. Also referred to as plateau keys or table keys. The two groups of keys are known as plateaus or tables.

**Transposing instruments**
On a transposing instrument, the note that sounds (concert pitch) is different from the one you finger. A fingered C on an alto sax sounds an E♭ concert pitch; a fingered C on a tenor saxophone sounds a B♭. Nontransposing instruments (violins, the piano, and the concert flute, for example) play in concert pitch.

**Tuning**
Adjusting the position of the mouthpiece so that the instrument plays at the correct pitch – in tune with other instruments, and with itself.

**Tuning cork**
Cork sleeve at the end of the neck. Also referred to as neck cork.

**U-bend**
The bow between body and bell.

**Wedge**
A 'bump' on the inside of the mouthpiece, making for a more aggressive, piercing sound. Also known as baffle.

**Window**

The rectangular opening of the mouthpiece, covered by the reed that is attached to it.

**Woodwind instrument**

Saxophones belong to the family of woodwind instruments, even though they're made of metal.

# TIPCODE LIST

The Tipcodes in this book offer easy access to short movies, photo series, soundtracks, and other additional information at www.tipbook.com. For your convenience, the Tipcodes in this Tipbook have been listed below.

| Tipcode | Topic | Page | Chapter |
|---|---|---|---|
| SAX-001 | Alto and tenor | 3 | 1 |
| SAX-002 | Octave key | 15 | 2 |
| SAX-003 | Three registers (alto) | 19 | 2 |
| SAX-004 | Soprano fantasy | 22 | 3 |
| SAX-005 | Alto fantasy | 23 | 3 |
| SAX-006 | Tenor fantasy | 24 | 3 |
| SAX-007 | Baritone fantasy | 25 | 3 |
| SAX-008 | The saxophone's range (alto) | 26 | 3 |
| SAX-009 | Same notes, different voices | 26 | 3 |
| SAX-010 | C5 on four saxes | 27 | 3 |
| SAX-011 | Checking rods and keys | 77 | 6 |
| SAX-012 | Adjusting underside reed | 109 | 8 |
| SAX-013 | Cutting a reed | 110 | 8 |
| SAX-014 | Using reed rush | 110 | 8 |
| SAX-015 | Attaching reed to mouthpiece | 117 | 9 |
| SAX-016 | A=440 | 119 | 9 |
| SAX-017 | Tuning fork | 120 | 9 |
| SAX-018 | Tuning | 121 | 9 |
| SAX-019 | Cleaning a pad | 139 | 10 |
| SAX-020 | A plastic saxophone | 150 | 12 |
| SAX-021 | Clarinet | 151 | 12 |
| SAX-022 | Oboe and bassoon | 152 | 12 |
| SAX-023 | Flute | 154 | 12 |
| SAX-024 | Making reeds | 159 | 13 |

**176**

# Want to know more?

*Tipbooks supply you with basic information on the instrument of your choice, and everything that comes with it. Of course there's a lot more to be found on all subjects you came across on these pages. This section offers a selection of magazines, books, helpful websites, and organizations.*

## MAGAZINES

Some magazines that offer additional information on saxophones and/or saxophone playing:

- *The Saxophone Journal*, www.dornpub.com/saxophonejournal.html

- *Windplayer*, www.windplayer.com

- Most saxophonists' organizations have their own publications (see page 180).

## BOOKS

Most books listed below cover the instrument itself and often discuss other subjects such as playing techniques, history, and repertoire at greater length.

- *The Art of Saxophone Playing*, by Larry Teal (Summy Birchard Inc., New Jersey, USA, 1963; 111 pages; ISBN 0-87487-057-7)

- *The Devil's Horn*: The Story of the Saxophone, from Noisy Novelty to King of Cool, by Michael Segell (Picador, 2006; 336 pages; ISBN 0-31242-557-0)

- *Saxophone – Yehudi Menuhin Music Guides*, by Paul Harvey (Kahn & Averill, London, 1995; 149 pages; ISBN 1-87108-253-6)

- *The Cambridge Companion to the Saxophone*, by Richard Ingham (Cambridge University Press, 1999; 242 pages; ISBN 0-52159-666-1).

- *Celebrating the Saxophone*, by Paul Lindemeyer (Hearst Books, published by William Morrow & Co., Inc. 1996; 96 pages; ISBN 0-68813-518-8)

- *The Saxophone*, by Lawrence Gwozdz (Egon Publishers, England, 1987; ISBN 0-90585-840-9). A translation of the first comprehensive treatise on the instrument, Das Saxophon, by Jaap Kool, first published in 1931.

- *Jean-Marie Londeix: Master of the Modern Saxophone*, by James C. Umble (Roncorp Publications, 2000; 660 pages; ISBN 0-93910-306-0)

### On reeds
Various books deal with reeds and reed adjustment only. Some examples:

- *Perfect a Reed ... and Beyond*, by Ben Armato (private publication; 1996; 43 pages; available at major US music dealers)

- *The Saxophone Reed, The Advanced Art of Adjusting Single Reeds*, by Ray Reed (Infinity Publishing, 2004; 215 pages, ISBN 0-74142-305-7)

- *Selection, Adjustment, and Care of Single Reeds*, by Larry Guy (Rivernote Press; 57 pages)

- *The Single Reed Adjustment Manual*, by Fred Ormand (Amilcare Publications, 2000; 84 pages)

- There's also a DVD on the subject: *Working the Single Reed*, by David Bourque (BCL Enterprises, 2005)

### Adolphe Sax
If you want to find out more about the instrument's inventor, check out the following books:

- *Adolphe Sax 1814–1894 — His Life and Legacy*, by Wally Horwood (Egon Publishers, England, 1980; 214 pages; ISBN 0-90585-818-2)

- *Sax and His Saxophone*, by Leon Kochnitzky (University of Louisville; 1985; ISBN 9-9910-832-6)

### More Tipbooks
Other Tipbooks that might be of interest for sax players are:

- *Tipbook Music on Paper – Basic Theory*

- *Tipbook Amplifiers and Effects*

- *Tipbook Clarinet*

- *Tipbook Flute and Piccolo*

Please see pages 217–221 to learn more about these and other Tipbook publications.

**179**

## SAXOPHONISTS' ORGANIZATIONS

Magazines and newsletters are also published by various national and international saxophonists' organizations. These organizations promote saxophone playing by organizing workshops and congresses (*e.g.*, the international World Saxophone Congress, as well as national congresses and conferences), and by providing information, establishing contacts between players at all levels, and so on.

* The North American Saxophone Alliance (NASA; www.saxalliance.org) publishes NASA Update and The Saxophone Symposium. For membership information: membership@saxalliance.org.

* The European Clarinet and Saxophone Society (www.eurocass.org) publishes Eurocass Magazine.

* The Clarinet and Saxophone Society of Great Britain (www.clarinetandsaxophone.co.uk) publishes Clarinet & Saxophone magazine

* The Queensland Clarinet & Saxophone Society (enquiries@ clarinetsaxophone.asn.au, www.clarinet-saxophone.asn.au) publishes The Australian Clarinet & Saxophone Magazine.

* The Clarinet and Saxophone Society of Victoria Inc., www.clasax.org.

## INTERNET

The Internet offers lots of advice and information about saxes, players, reeds, mouthpieces, and more. The following sites are some good starting points, offering both information and links to other sites.

* The International Saxophone Home Page (ISHP; also features the Saxophone Buyer's Guide by Webmaster Jason DuMars): www.saxophone.org

* The Saxophone Site (Sax on the Web): www.saxontheweb.net

* The Saxophone Shed: www.saxshed.com

* Sax Appeal: www.geocities.com/BourbonStreet/Delta/9590

- Bubba's Saxophone Links:
  www.mindspring.com/~mgm/saxlinks.html

### And more

- Find out everything about saxophone acoustics at
  www.phys.unsw.edu.au/~jw/saxacoustics.html.

- The Woodwind Fingering Guide offers all basic and
  numerous alternate fingerings for all saxophone voices at
  www.wfg.woodwind.org/sax.

- For frequently asked questions, check out
  www.bobrk.com/saxfaq.

### LOOKING FOR A TEACHER?

The Internet can also help you find a teacher. You may try to
search for "saxophone teacher" and the name of area or city
where you live, or visit one of the following special interest
websites:

- PrivateLessons.com: www.privatelessons.com

- MusicStaff.com: www.musicstaff.com

- The Music Teachers List: www.teachlist.com

- Private Music Instructor National Directory:
  www.oberwerk.com/pmind

# Tipbook fingering charts

On the following pages, you'll find extensive fingering charts for the soprano, alto, tenor, and baritone saxophone. Each double page shows fingerings for a single note in all registers and octaves, including toptones. Alternate or false fingerings are available as well. An interactive variation on this chapter can be found at www.tipbook.com.

### Key names

The illustration on the opposite page links the saxophone's keys to the keys in the charts. The keys have been identified according to the system of Jean Marie Londeix (see page 10).

### One note, all octaves

Each double page in this section shows the fingerings for one note in all registers of the instrument, indicating both the written note and its enharmonic equivalent (*e.g.*, Ab/G#).

### Registers

The instrument's range has been divided into four registers:

* low register: A3 or Bb3 to C#5

* middle register: D5 to C#6

* high register: D6 to F#6

* toptones (altissimo register): E6 to G7

*The instrument's four registers.*

### Octaves

The notes have been numbered to show the octave they're in (middle C = C4; the C one octave up, third-space C, is C5 — etcetera).

### Alternate fingerings

Many notes can also be played using one or more *alternate fingerings* or *false fingerings*.
Alternate fingerings are used for three purposes.

184

* They can make technical passages easier to play.

X
1
P
2
3

C2
C1
C4

C3
Tc
Ta
C5
Tf
D#
7

4
5
6

X
1
P
2
3

C2
C1
C4

C3
Tc
Ta
C5
Tf
D#
7

4
5
6

0

G#
C#
8
B♭

0

G#
C#
8
B♭

- They can be used to adjust the pitch of certain tones.

- They can be used to alter the timbre of a tone.

Note that the the difference between regular or basic and alternate fingerings is arbitrary; what some consider basic fingerings, others think of as alternate fingerings.

### Fingerings and voices
The letters S (soprano), A (alto), T (tenor), and/or B (baritone) at each fingering mark the saxophone voice(s) the fingering can be used for. Do note that the exact effect of some fingerings may differ per individual instrument, *e.g.*, one fingering may sound great on one alto, and less good on another.

### There's more
Rather than presenting *all* possible fingerings, the following pages show all basic fingerings and a selection of alternate fingerings that are of greater practical use. These fingering charts were supplied by Dutch saxophone master and collector Leo van Oostrom, who has one final tip: 'Also try playing toptones without the octave key: You'll find that this may improve either the pitch, the timbre, or the resonance of quite a few of these tones.'

# A

## Low register

### A3

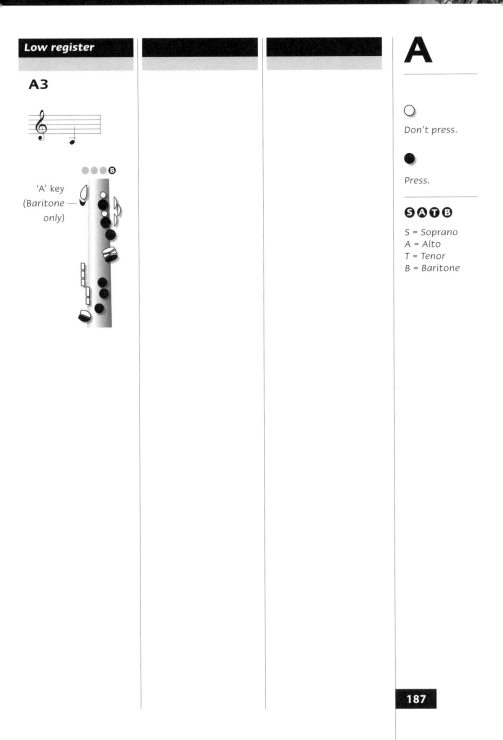

'A' key
(Baritone —
only)

○

Don't press.

●

Press.

**S A T B**

S = Soprano
A = Alto
T = Tenor
B = Baritone

# B♭

Enharmonic: A♯

○
Don't press.

●
Press.

---

Ⓢ

S = Soprano
A = Alto
T = Tenor
B = Baritone

| Low register | Low register | Middle register |
|---|---|---|
| **B♭3** | **B♭4** | **B♭5** |

**Low register**
Alternate fingerings

B♭4

**Middle register**
Alternate fingerings

B♭5

**Toptones**

B♭6

# B♭

*Enharmonic:* **A♯**

○
*Don't press.*

●
*Press.*

**S A T B**

S = Soprano
A = Alto
T = Tenor
B = Baritone

189

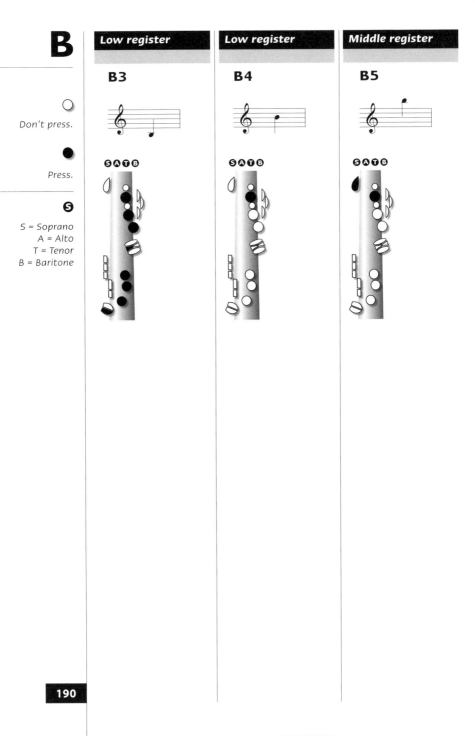

# B

### B3

### B4

### B5

Don't press.

Press.

S

S = Soprano
A = Alto
T = Tenor
B = Baritone

SATB

SATB

SATB

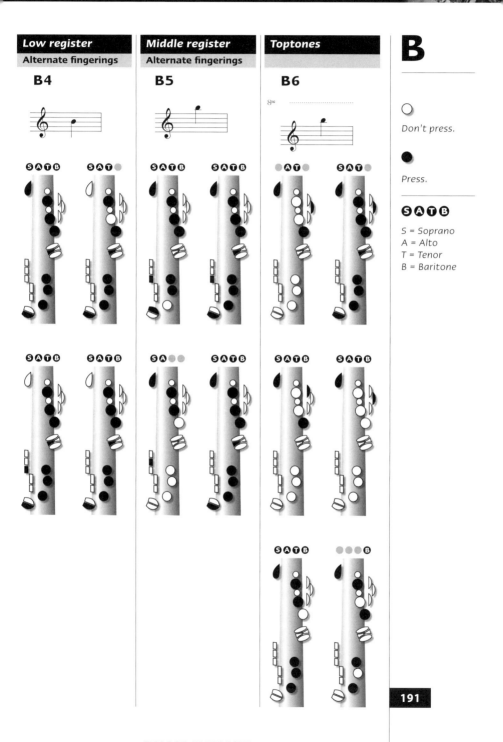

**Low register**
Alternate fingerings

**B4**

**Middle register**
Alternate fingerings

**B5**

**Toptones**

**B6**

**B**

○
Don't press.

●
Press.

Ⓢ Ⓐ Ⓣ Ⓑ

S = Soprano
A = Alto
T = Tenor
B = Baritone

# C

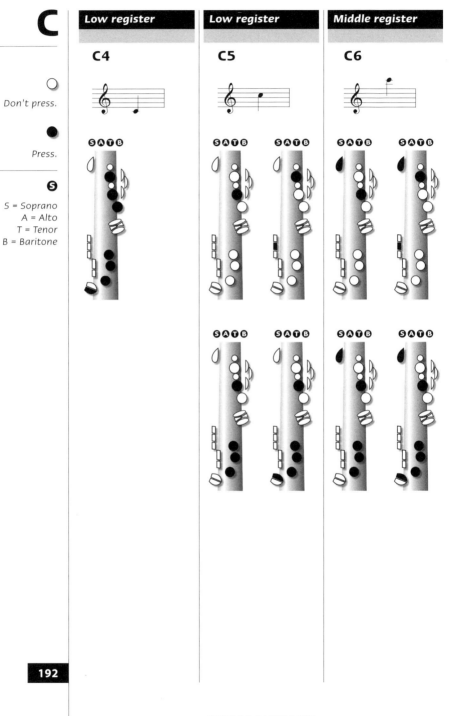

Don't press.

Press.

**S**

S = Soprano
A = Alto
T = Tenor
B = Baritone

| Low register | Low register | Middle register |
|---|---|---|
| C4 | C5 | C6 |

**Low register**
Alternate fingerings
**C5**

**Middle register**
Alternate fingerings
**C6**

**Toptones**
**C7**

# C

◯
*Don't press.*

●
*Press.*

🅢🅐🅣🅑

S = Soprano
A = Alto
T = Tenor
B = Baritone

193

# C♯

Enharmonic: **D♭**

○
Don't press.

●
Press.

**S**

S = Soprano
A = Alto
T = Tenor
B = Baritone

| Low register | Low register | Middle register |
|---|---|---|

## C♯4

## C♯5

## C♯6

## Low register
### Alternate fingerings
**C#5**

## Middle register
### Alternate fingerings
**C#6**

## Toptones
**C#7**

# C#

*Enharmonic:* **D♭**

○

*Don't press.*

●

*Press.*

**S A T B**

S = Soprano
A = Alto
T = Tenor
B = Baritone

**S A T B**    **S A T B**

**S A T B**    **S A T B**

**S A T B**    **S A T B**

**S A T B**    **S A T B**

**S A T B**    **S A T B**

**195**

# D

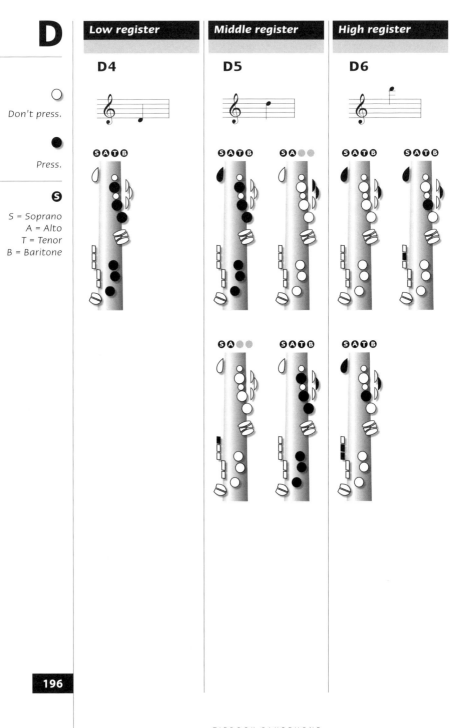

Don't press.

Press.

**S**

S = Soprano
A = Alto
T = Tenor
B = Baritone

**Low register**

**D4**

**Middle register**

**D5**

**High register**

**D6**

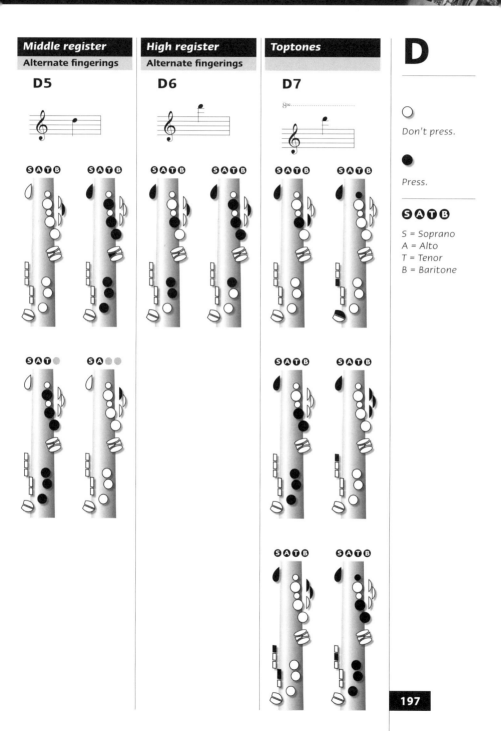

**Middle register**
Alternate fingerings

**D5**

**High register**
Alternate fingerings

**D6**

**Toptones**

**D7**

# D

○
*Don't press.*

●
*Press.*

**S A T B**

S = Soprano
A = Alto
T = Tenor
B = Baritone

# E♭

*Enharmonic:* **D♯**

*Don't press.*

*Press.*

**S**

S = Soprano
A = Alto
T = Tenor
B = Baritone

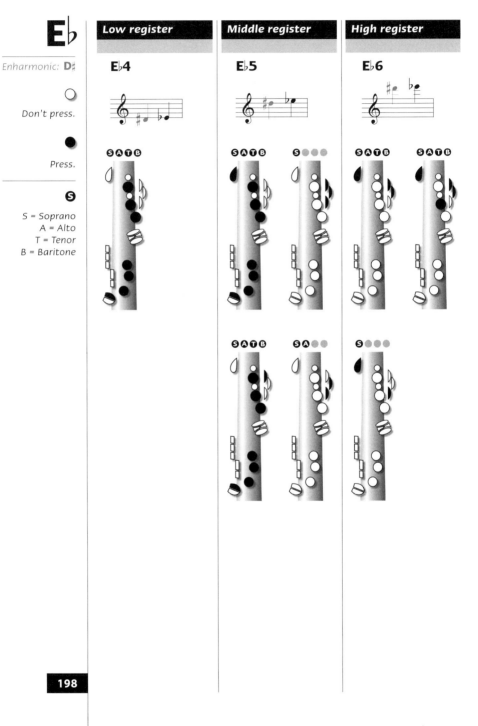

**Low register**

**E♭4**

**Middle register**

**E♭5**

**High register**

**E♭6**

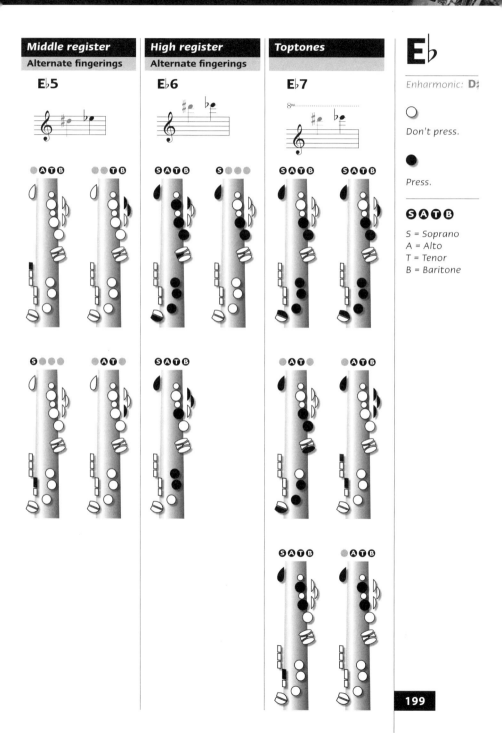

**Middle register**
Alternate fingerings

E♭5

**High register**
Alternate fingerings

E♭6

**Toptones**

E♭7

E♭

*Enharmonic:* **D♯**

○
*Don't press.*

●
*Press.*

**S A T B**

S = Soprano
A = Alto
T = Tenor
B = Baritone

# E

Low register | Middle register | High register

E4 | E5 | E6

Don't press. (open circle)

Press. (filled circle)

S

S = Soprano
A = Alto
T = Tenor
B = Baritone

**Middle register**
Alternate fingerings

**E5**

**High register**
Alternate fingerings

**E6**

**Toptones**

**E7**

**E**

○
*Don't press.*

●
*Press.*

🅢🅐🅣🅑

S = Soprano
A = Alto
T = Tenor
B = Baritone

**F**

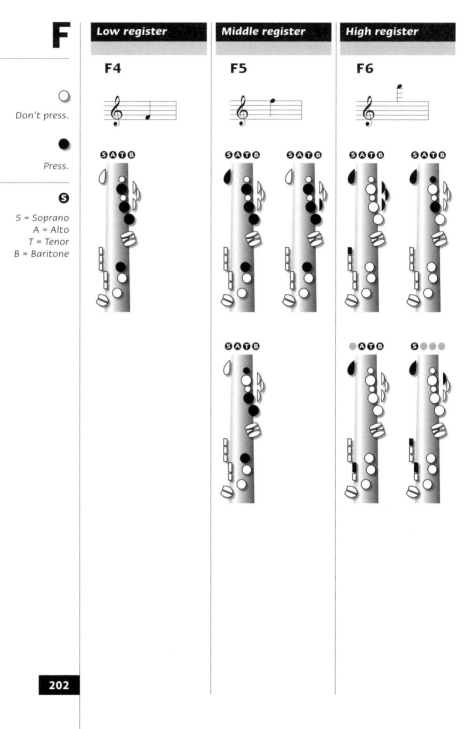

| Low register | Middle register | High register |
| --- | --- | --- |
| F4 | F5 | F6 |

Don't press.

Press.

S

S = Soprano
A = Alto
T = Tenor
B = Baritone

| Middle register | High register | Toptones | **F** |
| Alternate fingerings | Alternate fingerings | | |

**F5**

**F6**

**F7**

○ Don't press.

● Press.

🅢🅐🅣🅑

S = Soprano
A = Alto
T = Tenor
B = Baritone

# F♯

Enharmonic: **G♭**

○
Don't press.

●
Press.

**S**

S = Soprano
A = Alto
T = Tenor
B = Baritone

| Low register | Middle register | High register |
|---|---|---|
| **F♯4** | **F♯5** | **F♯6** |

204

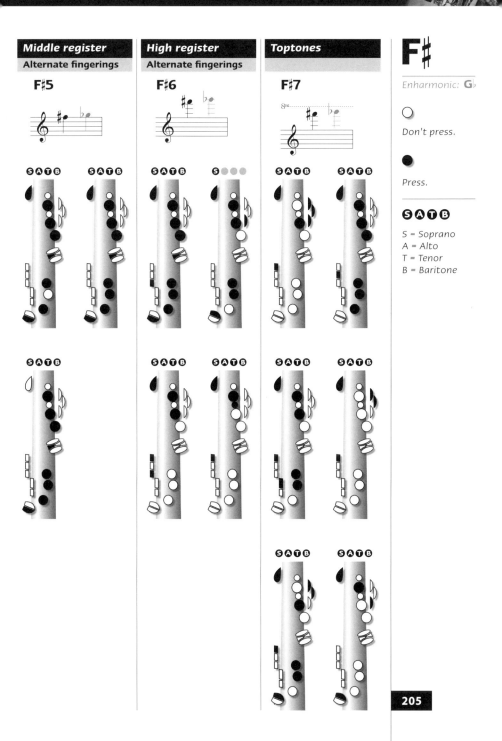

Middle register
Alternate fingerings
F♯5

High register
Alternate fingerings
F♯6

Toptones
F♯7

# F♯

*Enharmonic:* **G♭**

○

*Don't press.*

●

*Press.*

**S A T B**

S = Soprano
A = Alto
T = Tenor
B = Baritone

# G

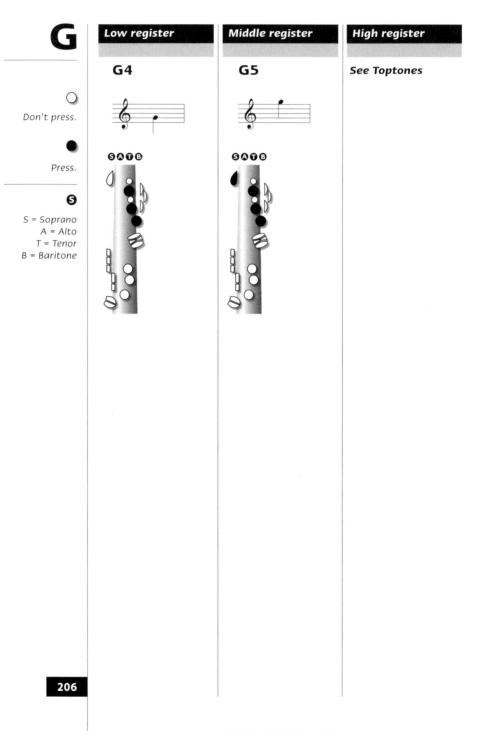

| Low register | Middle register | High register |
|---|---|---|
| **G4** | **G5** | *See Toptones* |

○
*Don't press.*

●
*Press.*

S

S = Soprano
A = Alto
T = Tenor
B = Baritone

## Low register
### Alternate fingerings
**G4**

## Middle register
### Alternate fingerings
**G5**

## Toptones
**G6**

# G

○ Don't press.

● Press.

⑤ⓐⓉⒷ

S = Soprano
A = Alto
T = Tenor
B = Baritone

# A♭

*Enharmonic:* **G♯**

○
*Don't press.*

●
*Press.*

**S**

S = Soprano
A = Alto
T = Tenor
B = Baritone

| Low register | Middle register | High register |
|---|---|---|
| **A♭4** | **A♭5** | *See Toptones* |

# A♭

Enharmonic: G♯

| Low register | Middle register | Toptones |
|---|---|---|
| **Alternate fingerings** | **Alternate fingerings** | |
| A♭4 | A♭5 | A♭6 |

Enharmonic: G♯

○

Don't press.

●

Press.

**S A T B**

S = Soprano
A = Alto
T = Tenor
B = Baritone

# A

## A4

## A5

*See Toptones*

○
*Don't press.*

●
*Press.*

**S**

S = Soprano
A = Alto
T = Tenor
B = Baritone

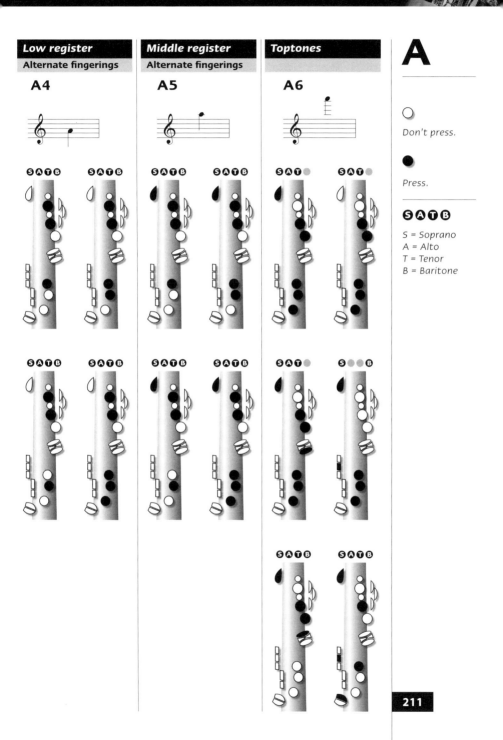

## A

### Low register
**Alternate fingerings**

**A4**

### Middle register
**Alternate fingerings**

**A5**

### Toptones

**A6**

○ Don't press.

● Press.

**S A T B**

S = Soprano
A = Alto
T = Tenor
B = Baritone

# ESSENTIAL DATA

*In the event of your instrument being stolen or lost, or if you decide to sell it, it's useful to have all the relevant data at hand. Here are two pages to list everything you need — for the insurance, for the police, for a prospective buyer or just for yourself.*

### INSURANCE

Company:

Phone:                       Website:

Agent:

Phone:                       Website:

Email:

Policy number:              Premium:

Instrument and accessories

Brand and type:

Serial number:               Price:

Date of purchase:

Purchased from:

Phone:                       Website:

Email:

Brand and type:

Serial number:               Price:

Place of purchase:

Purchased from:

Phone:                       Website:

Email:

### MOUTHPIECES

Brand and type:

Date of purchase:          Price:

Purchased from:

Phone:                       Website:

**212**

Email:

Brand and type:

Date of purchase:          Price:

Purchased from:

Phone:          Website:

Email:

**REEDS**

Brand, type, number:

Price:

Comments:

Brand, type, number:

Price:

Comments:

Brand, type, number:

Price:

Comments:

Brand, type, number:

Price:

Comments:

Brand, type, number:

Price:

Comments:

**ADDITIONAL NOTES**

# INDEX

*Please see the glossary on pages 169–175 for additional definitions of the terms used in this book.*

# THE TIPBOOK SERIES

*Did you enjoy Tipbook Saxophone? There are also Tipbooks for your fellow band and orchestra members! Tipbook Saxophone is just one of the many volumes of the international Tipbook Series. The series is comprised of eleven books on musical instruments, including the singing voice, in addition to Tipbook Music on Paper, Tipbook Amplifiers and Effects, and Tipbook Music for Kids and Teens – a Guide for Parents.*

*Every Tipbook is a highly accessible and easy-to-read compilation of the knowledge and expertise of numerous musicians, teachers, technicians, and other experts, written for musicians of all ages, at all levels, and in any style of music.*

### Tipbook Music on Paper

Tipbook Music on Paper – Basic Theory offers everything you need to read and understand the language of music. The book presumes no prior understanding of theory and begins with the basics, explaining standard notation, but moves on to advanced topics such as odd time signatures and transposing music in a fashion that makes things really easy to understand. It's also a handy reference, and the 4"x8" Tipbook format allows you to take it anywhere you go.

### Instrument Tipbooks

The Instrument Tipbooks each offer a wealth of highly accessible, yet well-founded information on one or more closely related instruments. The first chapters of each Tipbook explain the very basics of the instrument(s), explaining all the parts and what they do, describing what's involved in learning to play, and indicating typical instrument prices. The core chapters, addressed to advanced players as well, turn you into an instant expert on the instrument. This knowledge allows you to make an informed purchase and get the most out of your instrument. Comprehensive chapters on maintenance, intonation, and tuning are also included, as well a brief section on the history, the family, and the production of the instrument.

**217**

### Tipbook Violin and Viola, Tipbook Cello

The Tipbooks on orchestral strings cover a wide range of subjects, ranging from an explanation of different types of tuning pegs, fine tuners, and tailpieces, to how body dimensions and the bridge may influence the instrument's timbre. Tips on how to audition instruments and bows are included. Special chapters are dedicated to the characteristics of different types of strings, bows, and rosins, allowing you to get the most out of the instrument.

### Tipbook Piano

Choosing a piano becomes a lot easier with the knowledge provided in Tipbook Piano, which makes for a better understanding of this complex, expensive instrument without going into too much detail. How to judge and compare piano keyboards and pedals, the influence of the instrument's dimensions, different types of cabinets, how to judge an instrument's timbre, the difference between laminated and solid wood soundboards, accessories, hybrid and digital pianos, and why tuning and regulation are so important: Everything is covered in this handy guide.

### Tipbook Acoustic Guitar

Tipbook Acoustic Guitar explains all elements you recognize and judge a guitar's timbre, performance, and playability. Of course there are dedicated chapters on different types of strings and their characteristics, on changing and cleaning strings, on tuning, and even on how to best maintain your fingernails.

### Tipbook Electric Guitar & Bass Guitar

Electric guitars and bass guitars come in many shapes and sizes. Tipbook Electric Guitar & Bass Guitar explains all their features and characteristics, from neck profiles, frets, and types of wood to different types of pickups, tuning machines, and — of course — strings. Tuning and advanced do-it-yourself intonation techniques are included.

### Tipbook Flute & Piccolo

Flute prices range from a few hundred to fifty thousand dollars and more. Tipbook Flute and Piccolo tells you how workmanship, materials, and other elements make for different instruments with vastly different prices, and teaches you how to find the instrument that best suits your or your child's needs. Open-hole or closed-hole keys, a B-foot or a C-foot, split-E or donut, inline or offset G? You'll be able to answer all these questions — and more — after reading this guide.

### Tipbook Clarinet

Tipbook Clarinet sheds light on every element of this fascinating instrument. The knowledge presented in this guide makes that make for a good instrument, and helps selecting and auditioning a clarinet much easier, and you will be an instant expert on the pros and cons of offset and in-line trill keys, rounded or French-style keys, and all other aspects of the instrument. Special chapters are dedicated to reeds (selecting, testing, and adjusting reeds), mouthpieces and ligatures, and maintenance.

### Tipbook Trumpet & Trombone, Flugelhorn & Cornet

The Tipbook on brass instruments focuses on the smaller horns listed in the title. It explains all jargon you come across when you're out to buy or rent an instrument, from bell material to the shape of the bore, the leadpipe, valves and valve slides, and all other elements of the horn. Mouthpieces, a crucial choice for the sound and playability of all brasswinds, are covered in a separate chapter.

### Tipbook Keyboard & Digital Piano

Buying a home keyboard or a digital piano may find you confronted with numerous unfamiliar terms. Tipbook Keyboard & Digital Piano explains all of them in a very easy-to-read fashion — from hammer action and non-weighted keys to MIDI, layers and splits, arpeggiators and sequencers, expression

**219**

pedals and multi-switches, and more, including special chapters on how to judge the instrument's sound, accompaniment systems, and the various types of connections these instruments offer.

### Tipbook Drums

A drum is a drum is a drum? Not true — and Tipbook Drums tells you all the ins and outs of their differences, from the type of wood to the dimensions of the shell, the shape of the bearing edge, and the drum's hardware. Special chapters discuss selecting drum sticks, drum heads, and cymbals. Tuning and muffling, two techniques a drummer must master to make the instrument sound as good as it can, are covered in detail, providing step-by-step instructions.

### Tipbook Vocals – The Singing Voice

Tipbook Vocals –The Singing Voice helps you realize the full potential of your singing voice. The book, written in close collaboration with classical and non-classical singers and teachers, allows you to discover the world's most personal and precious instrument without reminding you of anatomy class. Topics include breathing and breath support, singing loudly without hurting your voice, singing in tune, the timbre of your voice, articulation, registers and ranges, memorizing lyrics, and more. The main purpose of the dedicated chapter on voice care is to prevent negative symptoms.

### Tipbook Amplifiers & Effects

Whether you need a guitar amp, a sound system, a multi-effects unit for a bass guitar, or a keyboard amplifier, Tipbook Amplifiers & Effects helps you make a good choice. Two chapters explain general features (controls, equalizers, speakers, MIDI, etc.) and figures (watts, ohms, impedance, etc.), and further chapters cover the specifics of guitar amps, bass amps, keyboard amps, acoustic amps, and sound systems. Effects and effect units are dealt with in detail, and there are dedicated chapters on microphones and pickups, and cables and wireless systems.

## Tipbook Music for Kids and Teens – a Guide for Parents

How do you inspire children to play music? How do you inspire them to practice? What can you do to help them select an instrument, to reduce stage fright, or to practice effectively? What can you do to make practice fun? How do you reduce sound levels and prevent hearing damage? These and many more questions are dealt with in Tipbook Music for Kids and Teens – a Guide for Parents and Caregivers. The book addresses all subjects related to the musical education of children from pre-birth to pre-adulthood, covering phases of musical development, learning styles, instrument selection, assessing a music teacher, practicing, guidance and motivation, and much more.

## International editions

The Tipbook Series is also available in Spanish, French, German, Dutch, Swedish, and (as of 2007) Chinese.

# TIPBOOK SERIES
# MUSIC AND MUSICAL
# INSTRUMENTS

| | |
|---|---|
| Tipbook Acoustic Guitar | *ISBN 90-76192-37-5* |
| Tipbook Amplifiers & Effects | *ISBN 90-76192-40-5* |
| Tipbook Cello | *ISBN 90-76192-47-2* |
| Tipbook Clarinet | *ISBN 90-76192-46 4* |
| Tipbook Drums | *ISBN 90-8767-102-4* |
| Tipbook Electric Guitar & Bass Guitar | *ISBN 90-76192-35-9* |
| Tipbook Flute & Piccolo | *ISBN 90-76192-42-1* |
| Tipbook Home Keyboard & Digital Piano | *ISBN 90-76192-31-6* |
| Tipbook Music for Kids and Teens | *ISBN 90-76192-50-2* |
| Tipbook Music on Paper | *ISBN 90-76192-32-4* |
| Tipbook Piano | *ISBN 90-76192-36-7* |
| Tipbook Saxophone | *ISBN 90-8767-101-6* |
| Tipbook Trumpet & Trombone | *ISBN 90-76192-41-3* |
| Tipbook Violin & Viola | *ISBN 90-76192-39-1* |
| Tipbook Vocals | *ISBN 90-76192-38-3* |

**Check www.tipbook.com for additional information!**